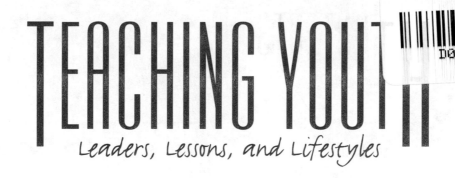

TEACHING YOUTH
Leaders, Lessons, and Lifestyles

RICHARD BARNES

ALLEN JACKSON

LifeWay Press
Nashville, Tennessee

Copyright 2000 • LifeWay Press
All rights reserved
ISBN 0-6330-0844-3
This book is a resource for courses numbered LS-0027, LS0056, LS 0106
for the ministry area "Sunday School Leadership" of the Christian Growth Study Plan.

Dewey Decimal Classification number 268.433
Subject Headings:
SUNDAY SCHOOLS—YOUTH
CHRISTIAN EDUCATION
BIBLE—STUDY AND TEACHING

Printed in the United States of America
Available from Customer Service Center 1-800-458-2772 and LifeWay Christian Stores

Youth Ministry Services Section
Youth Sunday School Ministry Department
Sunday School Group
LifeWay Christian Resources of the Southern Baptist Convention
127 Ninth Avenue, North
Nashville, Tennessee 37234-0174

Acknowledgments: Scripture taken from the NEW AMERICAN STANDARD BIBLE,
© Copyright The Lockman Foundation, 1960, 1962, 1963, 1968,
1971, 1972, 1973, 1975, 1977, 1995 Used by permission.

Scripture marked NIV is from the Holy Bible, New International Version,
Copyright © 1973, 1978, 1984 by International Bible Society

Contents

2

THE WRITERS

RICHARD BARNES became a Christian during a youth-led revival when he was a senior in high school. Sensing God's call to vocational ministry, Richard graduated from Dallas Baptist University and Southwestern Baptist Theological Seminary. Since 1969 Richard's passion has been teaching teenagers the Bible, whether serving on church staffs in Hawaii, Connecticut, and Texas or writing and producing Bible study curriculum. He has also written youth discipleship materials and contributed to leadership training resources and books, including *Youth Sunday School for a New Century*, published in 1999.

Richard Barnes

Richard is the Director of the Youth Sunday School Ministry Department in LifeWay Church Resources. He and his wife Mary live in Franklin, Tennessee, where they both enjoy working with high school youth at First Baptist Church and hiking Tennessee trails.

ALLEN JACKSON is a Texan by birth, but spent significant growing-up years in Georgia, Mississippi, and Louisiana. A graduate of the University of Southern Mississippi and New Orleans Baptist Theological Seminary, Allen spent 15 years serving as youth minister in churches in Louisiana and Georgia.

Despite the fact that he can wiggle his ears and touch his nose with his tongue, he is married to Judi and they have two children—Aaron, 11, and Sarah, 8.

Allen Jackson

Allen has written extensively for youth publications and has authored two books—*Into Their Shoes,* and *Connected, Committed, and a Little Bit Crazy* (co-authored with Randy Johnson). He is Associate Professor of Youth Ministry at the New Orleans Baptist Theological Seminary and enjoys leading DiscipleNow weekends and teaching discipleship classes to keep in touch with what is challenging today's youth.

FOREWORD

BY BILL TAYLOR

Captioned beneath a photograph of a high school quarterback ready to receive the snap from center was this probing question: "Is his Bible study changing the way he plays the game?" It's a question every Youth Sunday School leader needs to ask—and answer.

Even with the proliferation of Bible study groups, a startling level of biblical illiteracy exists among believers. Many believers ignore biblical authority and are only nominally obedient to God. The way they think and live is not significantly different from non-believers.

To effect change we must teach for spiritual transformation. *Spiritual transformation is God's work of changing a believer into the likeness of Jesus by creating a new identity in Christ and by empowering a lifelong relationship of love, trust, and obedience to glorify God.* Teaching for spiritual transformation is concerned with helping people live to make a difference in the world around them.

In traveling across America the past five years, I have learned about many people whose lives have been transformed through an encounter with God's Word:

• A teenaged boy in Florida whose friend, along with his parents, placed their faith in Christ during a Student FAITH visit, all of which began when he gave his friend a copy of *essential connection* magazine and invited him to youth activities.

• A high school girl from Hawaii who copies verses from *essential connection* magazine, takes them to school, and shares them with friends. "Christian teens today," she wrote, "are up against the devil himself—not that he's any comparison to the Almighty God, but I believe that your magazine has helped many sleeping Christians wake up and answer the call to join the ranks."

• A Youth Sunday School department director in Tennessee who called to say after leading a Bible study on hell, "Two young men found Christ as a direct result of what we studied in Sunday School."

These people heard a Bible lesson, but they didn't stop there. They continued to interact with God's Truth, allowing it to change their lives.

This book is a resource in the Teaching for Spiritual Transformation Series. The series is designed to help you develop a Sunday School ministry that has a focus on teaching for spiritual transformation. Each book in the series provides specific help for leaders of a specific target group: general leaders, adults, young adults, youth, children, or preschoolers.

Teaching for spiritual transformation will yield thousands of believers who give their best service to Christ. Then when we are confronted with questions like the one above, we can reply: "Yes. His Bible study is changing the way he plays the game, for the Christ he encounters in Scripture is changing his life."

Bill Taylor

Bill L. Taylor, Director
Sunday School Group

TEACHING YOUTH IN THE 21ST CENTURY

EXTRA! EXTRA! READ ALL ABOUT IT!

Stories of famous newspaper reporters, both fictional and historical, are a lot of fun. The Watergate scandal of the Nixon era was exposed by Woodward and Bernstein of the *Washington Post*. Brenda Starr has reported faithfully in the comic pages for decades. Perhaps the most famous newspaper crew of all was the group that worked for the Daily Planet. The roster in the city room included mild-mannered Clark Kent, a.k.a. Superman; the beautiful and competent Lois Lane; and the ever-inquisitive Jimmy Olson. The trio inevitably got to the truth, sprinkling justice and the American way as they searched out the news. They also fought a little crime along the way. They got to the bottom of every story by asking the classic newspaper questions: *Why? who? what? when? where? how?*

This book is for all of the adults who work with youth in a teaching or ministry capacity. As a youth worker, you are constantly asking questions to get to the bottom of a need in a young person's life. You patiently engage in some investigative reporting to discover the truth of a situation and engage in some advice-giving or problem-solving ministry. As a Bible teacher (or director, or in any other capacity in youth ministry), your teaching ministry might follow the same line of questioning: *Why do I teach? Who do I teach? What do I teach? How do I teach?*

As we engage this new millennium, we enter a time that has never been more critical for teaching youth God's Word. The cost of discipleship for the generation born since 1982 may be the highest it's been for any generation. In the closing years of the 20th century, Christian youth have become public targets for their faith—from Paducah, Kentucky; to Littleton, Colorado; to Fort Worth, Texas. Countless other teenagers throughout the world have stood boldly for Christ. Indeed, this generation is taking Jesus' call to radical discipleship in Luke 9:23-24 very seriously. To quote a group of Tennessee teenagers shortly after the Wedgwood tragedy, "Jesus tells us that the gates of hell can't stop us, and we're claiming that promise." [1]

Thirty years ago Billy Graham wrote a book to address the Jesus Movement—a previous generation that was experiencing a fresh movement of God. In his book, *The Jesus Generation* published in 1971, Dr. Graham observed that the most pressing need of that generation of new believers was for Bible study and the disciplines of the Christian life. [2] As bold as today's generation has become in its witness, these young people are also looking for substance. Once youth have tasted the "milk" of the Word (1 Pet. 2:2), they grow hungry for the "meat" (Heb. 5:11-14). Now is the time to lead youth toward experiencing the transforming power of loving, trusting, and obeying God's Word.

At the same time, there are millions of youth who have yet to hear or read a single word from the pages of Scripture. The adversary would like for us to believe that secular teenagers could care less about God's Word. But both the Scriptures (Isa. 55:10-11; John 12:32) and experienced youth workers (ask anyone involved in the Student FAITH Sunday School Evangelism Strategy) tell us this lost generation is hungry for the Truth about God when presented with love and honesty!

Who will take God's Word to them? How can we utilize Bible study groups to teach youth the Truth that sets them free? Questions such as these are what this book will try to address. Where do we start?

A GREAT PLACE TO START—THE GREAT COMMISSION!

As teachers, we tend to want to jump right into the methods: *How do I teach these kids?* Whatever methods we employ, we should be teaching youth from a solid

As we engage this new millennium, we enter a time that has never been more critical for teaching youth God's Word.

foundation of biblical principles. Perhaps you have heard this maxim:

Methods are many, and principles are few.

Methods change, but principles never do.

Beginning with the principles found in the Great Commission, how will we define *teaching youth the Bible*?

Have you ever noticed that the Great Commission in Matthew 28:16-20 begins with the disciples' obedience and ends with Jesus calling them to teach for obedience? First, the disciples obeyed Jesus by going to the mountain where He had told them to go (v. 16). Then Jesus concluded by calling them to teach others to obey (v. 20). When the disciples saw Jesus, they worshiped Him even while others doubted. Jesus began by assuring them of His authority to call them to make disciples of all people groups—including every group and clique on every school campus and in every neighborhood in every city, town, and rural area!

The authority we have as teachers comes from Jesus' Great Commission. Looking at the New Testament, we see that there is one Great Commission for the church that functions in five areas with four eventual results. This principle is called the 1-5-4 Kingdom Principle for Church Growth.[3] Simply stated, the 1-5-4 Principle involves:

- 1 driving force for church growth: The Great Commission.
- 5 essential church functions for church growth:

    Evangelism.—The good news spoken by believers and lived out in their lives.

    Discipleship.—God's process for transforming His children into Christlikeness.

    Fellowship.—"Familyship," sharing the common life in Christ.

    Ministry.—Meeting another person's need in the name of Christ.

    Worship.—Any activity in which believers experience God in a spiritually transforming way.

- 4 results:

    Numerical Growth.—Brings new life and hope to a church and reminds us to be about our Father's business.

    Spiritual Growth.—We grow in our relationships to the point that Christ lives in and through us in a disciplined lifestyle of Christlike love.

    Ministries Expansion.—Utilizing the Holy Spirit's gifts to believers and opening doors for ministering to people.

    Missions Advance.—Praying, giving, supporting, and sending its members as the Lord directs.

As Chuck Gartman indicates in Chapter 1 of *Youth Sunday School for a New Century*,[4] Youth Sunday School has purpose as its leaders seek to lead and equip youth to evangelize youth and the adults who influence them, disciple teenagers in their relationship with God, guide youth to fellowship with each other as well as with the entire church, minister to teens and their families, and guide youth to worship both personally and corporately. In short, all youth Bible study groups should be expressions of the church's five functions of evangelism, discipleship, fellowship, ministry, and worship.

A NEW DEFINITION FOR SUNDAY SCHOOL

Sunday School is the foundational strategy in a local church for leading people to faith in the Lord Jesus Christ and for building Great Commission Christians through Bible study groups that engage people in evangelism, discipleship, fellowship, ministry, and worship.

What does it mean for Youth Sunday School to be the "foundational strategy" in a local church? Simply stated, Youth Sunday School is a seven-day-a-week strategy that provides support for all other church ministries. If other ministries are not present in your church, as the "foundational strategy" Youth Sunday School can provide the foundation to help start one or more additional ministries. Here are a few examples of how Youth Sunday School is a foundational strategy:

1. *Pastor and other church leadership.*—Youth Sunday School affirms the pastor as the primary leader in its ministry of building Great Commission Christians. Youth leaders seek to lead students to worship both personally and corporately, including encouragement to worship through the church's music ministry.

2. *Discipleship.*—Youth Sunday School provides foundational discipleship through Bible teaching for spiritual transformation. Sunday School leaders encourage youth to strengthen their Christian walk by going deeper in discipleship groups.

3. *Missions.*—Youth Sunday School provides opportunities for youth to be involved in ministry and mission projects as a continuation of Bible study. Leaders also encourage further involvement in missions through missions organizations and giving to support missions.

4. *Family ministry.*—Youth Sunday School operates as a supportive partner with parents, affirming the home as the center of biblical guidance. Youth leaders recognize that parents are to be the primary Bible teachers and disciplers of their youth and encourage families to participate in the church's ministries with families.

STRATEGIC PRINCIPLES FOR A NEW CENTURY

For Youth Sunday School to thrive in any century, it must be driven by biblical principles. Here are five principles to guide us into the new century:

1. The Principle of Foundational Evangelism

Sunday School is the foundational evangelism strategy of the church. Youth Sunday School emphasizes ongoing, open Bible study groups that reproduce new groups as the best long-term approach for building a ministry environment that encourages unsaved youth to come to faith in Christ, that assimilates new believers into the life of the church, and that encourages believers to lead others to Christ.

At the heart of the teaching strategy for Sunday School for a New Century is creating "open" Bible study groups for teaching both believers and unbelievers. Sunday School teachers should not assume that all participants have completed advanced preparation before the session. Instead, Bible study leaders must plan to introduce participants to biblical truth that can transform their lives during and after the session.

2. The Principle of Foundational Discipleship

Knowing God through Jesus is the first step of discipleship. Youth Sunday School is a seven-day-a-week strategy and Bible study is a foundational step of discipleship for involving teenagers in seeking the Kingdom of God and fulfilling the Great Commission. Leaders can help youth to continue focusing on the truth after the session through learner guides, devotional guides, and personal and family relationships. Participants will also have the opportunity to reinforce the truth on the following Sunday.

3. The Principle of Family Responsibility

Sunday School affirms the home as the center of biblical guidance. Through Adult Sunday School and Youth Sunday School resources, Youth Sunday School is committed to helping equip Christian parents, including single parents, to fulfill their responsibility as the primary Bible teachers and disciplers of their children.

Youth leaders recognize that parents are to be the primary Bible teachers and disciplers of their youth.

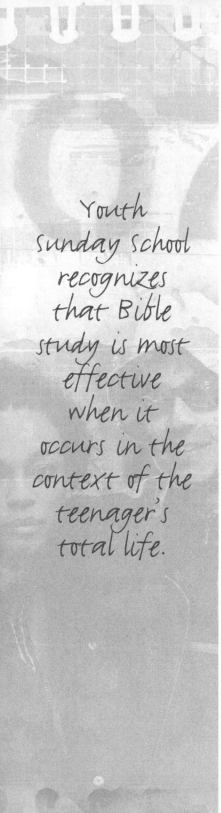

Youth sunday school recognizes that Bible study is most effective when it occurs in the context of the teenager's total life.

4. The Principle of Spiritual Transformation

Sunday School engages learners in the biblical process of instruction that leads to spiritual transformation. Spiritual transformation is God's work of changing a believer into the likeness of Jesus by creating a new identity in Christ and by empowering a lifelong relationship of love, trust, and obedience to glorify God. Youth Sunday School recognizes that Bible study is most effective when it occurs in the context of the teenager's total life, especially family relationships, and when it considers the special needs, generational perspective, age and life-stage characteristics, and learning styles of the individual youth.[5]

Beginning with fall 2000 resources, the design for teaching and learning is changing to a common format, preschool through adult, with three key words— *Prepare, Encounter,* and *Continue.* To begin, leaders *prepare* not only a lesson, but also themselves. Then leaders and learners *encounter* God's Word in the context of a Bible study group as together they acknowledge the authority of who is in charge of their lives, search the biblical Truth, discover the Truth, and personalize the Truth. And then they struggle with the Truth and decide whether to believe and obey the Truth as they *continue* to live and learn in daily relationships, especially in their families.

5. The Principle of Biblical Leadership

Sunday School calls leaders to follow the biblical standard of leadership. Youth Sunday School recognizes that the leader is the lesson and every leader is accountable for being an authentic example of Christianity in personal living and producing new leaders for service through the ministries of the church. Finally, Youth Sunday School recognizes that planning is essential to implementing its strategy.

CRITICAL QUESTIONS FOR THE NEW CENTURY

• Since Youth Sunday School has crossed the threshold into the 21st century, to what extent will God be able to work through its leaders (both youth and adults) and its participants to extend His kingdom?

• As God sends spiritual awakening in this generation, will Youth Sunday School leaders be *prepared* to lead youth to *encounter* God's Word in Bible study groups committed to *continue* learning and living for Christ daily in all relationships, including the family?

Every Bible study participant expects the teacher to come prepared to teach. What if youth came prepared to report on what God taught them and how God used them in ministry since the previous Bible study session? What if both adults and youth brought someone who needed to hear God's Word? Transforming lives through teaching God's Word is what this book will address. Transforming lives, though, begins with God's transforming us. Are we ready?

Endnotes

[1] "Satan, c/o Hell," an open letter to Satan by students named Garth Greer, Clint Razor, Courtney Thompson, Kyle Porter, Sarah Kristy, John Bray, Erin, Erica, Megan, Allison Woods, Paul Blair Bryant, and Jessica Kendall, September 1999.

[2] Billy Graham, *The Jesus Generation*, Grand Rapids: Zondervan, 1971, 21.

[3] Gene Mims. *Kingdom Principles for Church Growth*. Nashville: Convention Press, 1984.

[4] Chuck Gartman and Richard Barnes, *Youth Sunday School for a New Century*, Nashville: LifeWay Press, 1999. Available through LifeWay Christian Stores, 1-800-458-2772, or online at www.lifeway.com/order/index.asp.

[5] For an excellent study on spiritual transformation, see *Jesus By Heart* by Roy Edgemon and Barry Sneed, Nashville: LifeWay Press, 1999.

CHAPTER 1

WHY DO WE TEACH YOUTH?

"Then Jesus took His disciples up to the mountain, and gathering them around Him, He taught them saying:

> *Blessed are the meek*
> *Blessed are they that mourn*
> *Blessed are the merciful*
> *Blessed are they who thirst for justice*
> *Blessed are you when persecuted*
> *Blessed are you when you suffer*
> *Be glad and rejoice, for your reward is great in Heaven!*

Then Simon Peter said, "Do we have to write this down?"
And Andrew said, "Are we supposed to know this?"
And James said, "Will we have a test on this?"
And Philip said, "I don't have any paper."
And Bartholomew said, "Do we have to turn this in?"
And John said, "The other disciples didn't have to learn this!"
And Matthew said, "When do we get out of here?"
And Judas said, "What does this have to do with real life?"

Then one of the Pharisees present asked to see Jesus' lesson plans and inquired of Jesus, "Where are your terminal objectives in the cognitive domain?"

And Jesus wept.[1]

AND NOW FOR THE NEWS. . .

A newspaper reporter asks the question, *Why?* when he wants to get to the motivation of a story. Let's say there is a major story on an expedition to climb a mountain. A newspaper reporter treks through the famous mountains of the world—Mt. Fuji in Japan; Mt. Everest in Nepal; Stone Mountain in Georgia—in pursuit of a renowned climber. When the interview finally happens, it begins something like this: "Why, sir, did you climb the mountain?" The explorer answers, "Why, you ask, did I climb the mountain? Why? I climbed it because it was there!" The newspaper reporter could have asked several more *Why?* questions, both of the explorer and of himself for going all that way for that silly quote.

We cannot dismiss the *why* behind the teaching-learning event. In a later chapter, we will examine the *why* questions that take place as we help youth encounter the Bible and as we guide them to continue throughout the next week (and their lives). For now, our investigation centers upon the question, "Why do we teach youth?"

THE PREDICTABLE ADOLESCENT QUESTION

Why questions could have been asked of Jesus:

Why did He teach? Why did He choose to teach disciples? Why did He choose to teach us through the disciples and through the work of the biblical writers? Why did He have such incredible patience with His slow learners?

Perhaps some of the *wh*y that motivates adults to teach youth can be found by answering some of the questions about Jesus' teaching ministry. If we can capture the picture of Jesus as a transformational teacher, perhaps we can find some answers as to what might motivate us. The first word that we know about that Jesus spoke as a twelve-year-old boy was the word *why* (which is no surprise to any parent of an adolescent). Jesus had been taken to Jerusalem for the annual family trip for the Feast of the Passover. After the feast was over, Joseph and Mary assumed that Jesus had climbed into the minivan of one of their relatives for the trip home. This was not the case, and when they finally located Jesus–back in Jerusalem–here's what happened:

And it came about that after three days they found Him in the temple, sitting in the midst of the teachers, both listening to them, and asking them questions. And all who heard Him were amazed at His understanding and His answers. And when they saw Him, they were astonished; and His mother said to Him, "Son, why have You treated us this way? Behold, your father and I have been anxiously looking for you." And He said to them, "Why is it that you were looking for me? Did you not know that I had to be in My father's house?" Luke 2:46-49

There's a clue here: Jesus had to be in church, talking and sharing, teaching and being taught. His parents couldn't understand his urgency. I pray for my youth as you do for yours that they will have a sense of urgency about the teaching that takes place in God's house. From the start, Jesus had a sense of urgency about His teaching ministry. As a twelve-year old, He was in one of the preparation cycles of his lifelong lesson plan.

He was preparing the disciples (the twelve, the wider group that followed Him, and also ultimately us!) for a teaching ministry of their own. He *prepared* so they could *encounter,* and after His death and resurrection *continue* to have an effective ministry. Remember the italicized words in that last sentence. We will handle the concept throughout this book. In chapter 4, you will become more familiar with the *prepare, encounter, continue* formula.

FAITHFUL FIG TREES BEAR FINISHED FRUIT

As I write this particular chapter, I am sitting in Bethlehem. Not Bethlehem, Pennsylvania, but the real deal. I am on a tour, and I am absolutely blessed to be in the Holy Land. As a matter of fact, you will probably get tired of my references to the places where Jesus went, but I am overwhelmed by this experience. I have been like a newspaper reporter during the trip. *Why did Jesus do this? Who was He with? Where did it happen? What was the motivation?* (You can tell that I am in the mood for all of this investigative reporting.)

Earlier today, I went to Bethany where Mary, Martha, and Lazarus lived. I also saw a fig tree in the same area as the one that Jesus cursed. What? You aren't familiar with that story? OK, here's a reminder from Mark 11:13-14: *Seeing in the distance a fig tree in leaf, he went to find out if it had any fruit. When he reached it, he found nothing but leaves, because it was not the season for figs (v. 14). Then he said to the tree, "May no one ever eat fruit from you again"* (NIV)[2]. And his disciples heard him say it.

And now, the rest of the story (vv. 20-24):

In the morning, as they went along, they saw the fig tree withered from the roots. Peter remembered and said to Jesus, "Rabbi, look! The fig tree you cursed has withered!" "Have faith in God," Jesus answered. "I tell you the truth, if anyone says to this mountain, 'Go, throw yourself into the sea,' and does not doubt in his heart but believes that what he says will happen, it will be done for him. Therefore I tell you, ¹*whatever you ask for in prayer, believe that you have received it, and it will be yours.*

The truth here is that the fig tree that Jesus was looking at had buds, but no fruit. Further, it didn't even have the necessary "pre-fruit" or first fruit called *pagga* (pronounced, 'pag-ge-i'). In other words, it looked like a fruit-producing tree, but it was not going to bear any figs.

Some of the most interesting, yet puzzling, words of Jesus are the ones that make Him seem as if He was in a bad mood. One might wonder, *What did the poor fig tree ever do?* The answer seems to lie with the idea that faith is illustrated in a tree that looked like it was healthy, but wasn't. The *why?* of teaching youth is found in the idea that if we say we care about teenagers, we must teach. Faith in God's ability to work out the details in us is the mystery of letting go. We must do what we are designed to do—through faith obey God's direction in our lives. Here is another illustration: Jesus consistently had negative things to say about two groups of people—those who were so legalistic they did not help others, and those who would negatively affect the spiritual growth of a child. In three of the Gospels, Jesus emphatically makes the point that children (and youth) are special in His perspective:

- *And whoever receives one such child in My name receives Me; but whoever causes one of these little ones who believe in Me to stumble, it is better for him that a heavy millstone be hung around his neck, and that he be drowned in the depth of the sea.* (Matt 18:5-6).
- *And whoever causes one of these little ones who believe to stumble, it would be better for him if, with a heavy millstone hung around his neck, he had been cast into the sea.* (Mark 9:42).
- *And He said to His disciples, "It is inevitable that stumbling blocks should come, but woe to him through whom they come! It would be better for him if a millstone were hung around his neck and he were thrown into the sea, than that he should cause one of these little ones to stumble* (Luke 17:1-2).

The why? of teaching youth is found in the idea that if we say we care about teenagers, we must teach.

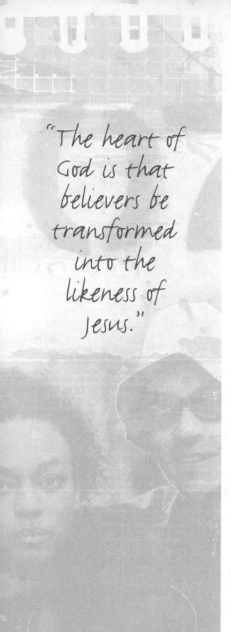

> "The heart of God is that believers be transformed into the likeness of Jesus."

While in Israel, I saw several millstones. They aren't pendants like you get in the gift shop at Six Flags. The millstone I saw was the size of a round dining room table, made of stone, with a hole in the center like a donut. I suppose the hole is for the serpentine chain to go around someone's neck (just kidding). If you had a millstone around your neck, you were going to sleep with the fishes. Jesus was serious.

What is the point? The point is that the major *why?* of teaching youth is that Jesus placed a premium on the instruction that is intended to be passed down from older to younger generations. He knew about the great Shema in Deuteronomy that placed emphasis on the flow of spiritual truth and spiritual lifestyle from one generation to the next.

Hear, O Israel! The LORD is our God, the LORD is one! And you shall love the LORD your God with all your heart and with all your soul and with all your might. And these words, which I am commanding you today, shall be on your heart; and you shall teach them diligently to your sons and shall talk of them when you sit in your house and when you walk by the way and when you lie down and when you rise up (Deut. 6:4-7).

Paul wrote to Timothy to "continue on in the things you have learned and become convinced of, knowing from whom you learned them" (2 Tim. 3:14). The reference is to the godly mother and grandmother who nurtured young Timothy's spiritual growth. They prepared themselves and their young man for faith and salvation through the Bible lessons (sacred writings) taught from his childhood.

SPIRITUAL TRANSFORMATION IS MEANT TO BE PASSED DOWN

I really like a quote that I read in a booklet about spiritual transformation. The words would make a great poster, "The heart of God is that believers be transformed into the likeness of Jesus."[3] The goal is the same for the Hebrew parents who memorized the Shema, for Paul as he wrote to Timothy, and for the multitudes of faithful adults who volunteer to work with youth on a weekly basis. Something has to be done to make the next generation "get it."

Another memorable quote that I heard when I was working with teachers in Winnfield, Louisiana, was offered by one of the wiser adult teachers in the church. Mrs. Bea Straughn used to say, "The conviction of one generation, if not communicated with passion can easily become the preference of the next. If that happens, it is mere opinion by the third generation." From conviction to opinion in three generations. Again the *why?* of teaching teenagers screams at us.

Sometime back, I was studying Dr. Luke's account of the Jesus story and I noticed an unusual amount of numbered groups in a relatively short span of verses. Beginning in Luke 9:1, we see Him calling the twelve together to give them "power and authority over all the demons and to heal diseases." After that, Jesus facilitated the miracle of the feeding of 5000 (v.12-17). Eight days later, He took Peter, James, and John to the mountains to witness another miracle. The three were privileged to see the vision of Moses, Elijah, and Jesus as Jesus was caught up in prayer.

The remainder of Luke 9 is a description of the ministry that Jesus had "along the way" (more about that in a minute) and then the reader reads the beginning of chapter 10:

Now after this the Lord appointed seventy others, and sent them two and two ahead of Him to every city and place where He Himself was going to come. And He was saying to them, "The harvest is plentiful, but the laborers are few; therefore beseech the Lord of the harvest to send out laborers into His harvest.

I don't make much of the numbers presented in the chapters except for the fact that along the way, Jesus involved people. (In Luke 10, NIV indicates that seventy-two were sent out). As He performed miracles, He involved people. As He prayed and worshiped, He involved people. As He prepared to evangelize the world, He involved people. Keep in mind that these accounts were fairly early in the ministry

of Jesus. He was preparing Himself and His disciples for the lessons that were ahead. Even the last thing that He said to them on earth suggested preparation for the lessons to come:

And Jesus came up and spoke to them, saying, "All authority has been given to Me in heaven and on earth. "Go therefore and make disciples of all the nations, baptizing them in the name of the Father and the Son and the Holy Spirit, teaching them to observe all that I commanded you; and lo, I am with you always, even to the end of the age (Matt. 28:18-20).

The word *Go* is better translated, "As you are going. . . ." As you are going, be an agent of spiritual transformation!

PREPARE, ENCOUNTER, CONTINUE

Even though we are saving the specifics of the *prepare, encounter, continue* formula for chapter 4, take a closer look at the teaching methodology of Jesus in the Scripture you just examined. Throughout Luke 9, you can pick up a pattern:

- Jesus prepared Himself for the lessons of the moment, then
- He prepared the disciples for what they would learn, then
- He taught the lesson using a variety of methodology—and finally
- He helped the hearers see how the lesson could and should be a part of their thinking and acting from then on.

Look at just a few of the cycles in chapter 9, using the various numbered groups with whom He ministered. He *prepared.*

And He called the twelve together, and gave them power and authority over all the demons, and to heal diseases (Luke 9:1).

He called the twelve together. An intense amount of prayer preceded the selection of the disciples. Back in Luke 6:12 you read that He spent the night in prayer, and then He chose twelve of the many followers to be apostles. In the days following their appointment as apostles, Jesus taught them many things including the beatitudes, love for friends and enemies, the essence of faith. He allowed them to witness miracles, spending time with Him and walking where He walked. Now He verbally empowers them to share in the lifestyle He has modeled. The leader has been the lesson and now He prepares them for the lesson at hand. This one is a life lesson.

He guided the twelve to *encounter* the truth:

And He sent them out to proclaim the kingdom of God, and to perform healing. And He said to them, "Take nothing for your journey, neither a staff, nor a bag, nor bread, nor money; and do not even have two tunics apiece. "And whatever house you enter, stay there, and take your leave from there. "And as for those who do not receive you, as you go out from that city, shake off the dust from your feet as a testimony against them (Luke 9:2-5).

Those guys had to be in shock. Now they were going to do the things they had seen Jesus do. There is no promise in this verse that He intended to accompany them. He was sending them away.

I haven't ever been skydiving, but my friend Dave Paxton has made about a gazillion jumps. He keeps promising to teach me. Well, I can read all about skydiving; I can watch Dave jump out of planes (it is not unusual for Dave to parachute into youth camp); I can take written tests on skydiving. But until I realize that I am going to have to do this myself, the lessons stay in my head and I don't necessarily sense a need to do anything constructive with the information. However, if I know from the beginning that I am eventually going to be pushed out of the plane, I will make sure that I don't doze off during parachute-packing class.

Part of the *why* of preparation is beginning with the idea that the lesson won't just lay on the table at the end of the session. The hearers will deal with the truth of the lesson and the teacher and the learners must grasp that eventually the lesson will take wings (or a parachute) and fly. I can only imagine that after Jesus said, "Boys it's time to go," that their ears perked up for the next few minutes of the lesson. He gave them specific instructions, explicitly expounding the truth.

And now the *continue* of the lesson seems to come naturally:

And departing, they began *going about among the villages, preaching the gospel, and healing everywhere* (Luke 9:6).

It is the desire of every one of us who has ever taught a Bible study to teenagers that they would enact the truth of the lesson so readily. I would imagine that questions were asked and I can imagine that they were not completely sure that it would work. (But we will save that for the *encounter* section of the book.) When the seventy returned in verse 17 of chapter 10, they almost seem surprised that the spiritual confrontations unfolded exactly as Jesus had taught them before He sent them. If you have taught youth before, you will recognize the flushed, excited look on their faces as the lesson becomes life for them as well.

TRANSFORMABLE TEACHERS TRANSFORMING TEENAGERS

The formula is not complicated. When we, as leaders, yield to the preparation that it takes to be an agent of transformation between God and teenagers, we see miracles happen. I grieve when I hear adults (sometimes pastors) say to youth ministers who invest in teacher training, "Those workers are just volunteers. They won't give you that much time in preparation." I know otherwise. God has called a group of caring adults to sit knee-to-knee with teenagers in Bible study and in life and they know intuitively that they cannot do it without preparing.

And that is the *Why?* of the story.

Endnotes

[1] Story making the rounds in cyberspace. I first saw it in *How Your Church Family Works*, by Peter L. Stenke.

[2] From the Holy Bible, *New International Version*, copyright© 1973, 1978, 1984 by International Bible Society.

[3] Booklet published by LifeWay Christian Resources, "Spiritual Transformation: Growing More Like Christ."

When we, as leaders, yield to the preparation that it takes to be an agent of transformation between God and teenagers, we see miracles happen.

WHO ARE THE YOUTH WE TEACH?

Investigative journalists—especially criminal reporters—are obsessed with the *Who?* question. Unsolved or disputed cases are especially intriguing. In the early part of this century, it was the kidnaping of the Lindbergh baby that captivated the attention of the nation. More recently, the media focused on O.J. Simpson's spectacular trial, the unsolved killing of JonBenet Ramsey, and lesser-known cases that appear in the pages of newspapers every day. People want to know the *who?* of the story. During O.J.'s trial, the strategy of the defense attorney, Johnnie Cochran, involved casting suspicion as to whether the prosecution had the right *who?* for the crime. ("If the glove doesn't fit, you must acquit.") The solving of the *who?* question is of utmost importance. It is essential to correctly identify the object of any investigation.

THE WHO? OF LUKE 9-10
As a practice exercise (OK, we don't have a Superman decoder ring), look again at the passage we considered earlier. In Luke 9-10, you will recall that Jesus co-ministered with at least four groups of people. In the spirit of our investigative reporting, we need to discuss who they were, and possibly if the *who?* affected the type of experience that Jesus had for them.

THE TWELVE
OK, journalists, take the first *who?* of Luke 9. The first group mentioned was "the Twelve." What do we know about them? From the Scripture, we know that they were a separate group from the larger body of disciples, named in Luke 6 and Mark 3. Don't get discouraged with the names. Sometimes they are called by different names. Peter is sometimes Simon or Cephas. Matthew is also called Levi and

Bartholomew and Nathaniel. Judas the Son of James is also called Thaddaeus. For now, let's agree that the Twelve were special messengers of Jesus Christ. We see here that He delegated authority to them for certain tasks. The word *apostle* is used of those twelve disciples whom Jesus sent out, two by two, during His ministry in Galilee to expand His own ministry of preaching and healing. It was on that occasion, evidently, that they were first called *apostles*. (See also Mark 3:14, 6:30.) Additional information (perhaps more than we need, but I will make a point in a minute) is provided by consulting a Bible dictionary:

The word *apostle* is sometimes used in the New Testament in a general sense of *messenger*. For instance, when delegates of Christian communities were charged with conveying those churches' contributions to a charitable fund, they were described by Paul as "messengers *apostles* of the churches" (2 Cor. 8:23). Jesus also used the word this way when He quoted the proverb, "A servant is not greater than his master, nor he who is sent [literally, "an apostle"] greater than he who sent him" (John 13:16). Jesus Himself is called "the Apostle . . . of our confession" (Heb. 3:1), a reference to His function as God's special Messenger to the world.[1]

I will not explore the *who?* of the other groups mentioned in these two chapters to this extent, but don't miss the point. As we prepare to help teenagers encounter the word, we need to research the *who?* of the Scripture as well as the *who?* of our class enrollment!

FIVE THOUSAND HUNGRY PEOPLE (ER, MEN)

After an interlude about Herod and John the Baptist and Elijah, (talk about a *who?* research project!) Dr. Luke tells us that the Twelve returned to report on the neat things that happened. Jesus took them for a little debriefing session to a town called Bethsaida on the north shore of the Sea of Galilee. As would be predictable with miracle workers, the crowds found Jesus, so He taught them. At the end of the day, Jesus instructed the disciples to feed the hungry people. Who were they?

First, the number was likely several times the five thousand that was reported. The Bible tells us that only the men were counted, and even that was an estimate (v. 14). Secondly, we know they were needy. There were some that were sick and Jesus healed them. They were hungry, both spiritually and physically. They were persistent. It was in a remote location (v. 12) and the crowd apparently pursued Jesus until they caught Him. John's account of this story introduces us to another of the *who?* persons of the day—a little boy who had a lunch he was willing to share.

If I know the teacher in you, you are ready to prepare a lesson right now on the spiritual implications of all these characters. Hold off for a few minutes—we have two more stories to investigate.

THREE MEN AND A TRANSFIGURATION

Now (whew!–still in the same chapter in Luke!) Jesus takes Peter, James, and John to a mountain (either Mt. Hermon or Mt. Tabor) for an incredibly special retreat experience. Why these three?[2] We don't know why He singled them out. Maybe they were more spiritually tuned in than the other nine. The words they heard Jesus say in the eight days between the feeding of the 5000 and the transfiguration were tough words, and their response was certainly favorable. Maybe it was because they were some of the first among the ones called (Luke 1:16). They were also present at some miracles that the others missed (Luke 8:51).

Additionally, James and John were sons of Zebedee. They were fishermen. They had reputations of having explosive personalities that led to their collective nickname, "The Sons of Thunder." A little research could reveal even more about this illustrious trio, but you get the idea. We didn't even look at the possibilities for researching Moses, Elijah, or even where Jesus was in His earthly ministry when this event happened. With a little effort, the *who?* can be investigated. But there is one more group from this passage to be studied.

SEVENTY SENT

After a few more meaningful moments in Luke, we meet another group into whom Jesus invested as the end of His earthly ministry drew near. He told the disciples of the suffering He would endure (9:21) and in verse 44, He told them of His death. He spoke of the commitment to discipleship in 9:51-62 as the completion of His ministry was at hand. Surely, some of those He would send out understood the urgency of their mission. We know they were part of the larger group of disciples, competent to prepare the towns for the upcoming visit that Jesus would make. We can guess that they were around when the disciples reported back, as the instructions that Jesus gave were similar. We have no indication that these 36 teams of 2 were otherwise remarkable. We know they had seen Jesus' power and they were willing to trust Him. The results speak for their faithfulness.

SO WHAT?

I'm sorry—I didn't mean to throw another question in on top of all the *whos?* What I mean by "so what?" is that it is a great practice exercise to investigate the characters in a couple of chapters in Luke. Remember, though, that we are talking about what it takes to prepare for the Bible study experience. In preparation, we can investigate all of the characters in the particular part of Scripture to be examined in a given week. Such research is helpful in bringing life to the truth of the passage. But we cannot let that be the only *who?* investigation that we conduct. We also have to prepare for the *who?* that refers to the students who may be in our classes.

The majority of this chapter will be given to studying the youth in our ministries, but we also need to consider the *who?* that is leading the class. Certainly a thorough study of Luke 9-10 would not overlook the Leader who was the Lesson. Jesus was a walking, talking example of the *who?* in Bible study!

So who are the adults who teach youth? An earlier book that I coauthored with Randy Johnson was entitled, *Connected, Committed, and a Little Bit Crazy*, and it was basically a love letter to all of the adult volunteers we had ever met. Let me share with you a short Bible study that has become a favorite of mine as I encourage adults who work with youth.

In Exodus 17-18, the leadership of Israel was definitely in the hands of Moses. A battle was going on between Israel and the Amelekites:

Then Amalek came and fought against Israel at Rephidim. So Moses said to Joshua, "Choose men for us, and go out, fight against Amalek. Tomorrow I will station myself on the top of the hill with the staff of God in my hand." And Joshua did as Moses told him, and fought against Amalek; and Moses, Aaron, and Hur went up to the top of the hill. So it came about when Moses held his hand up, that Israel prevailed, and when he let his hand down, Amalek prevailed. But Moses' hands were heavy. Then they took a stone and put it under him, and he sat on it; and Aaron and Hur supported his hands, one on one side and one on the other. Thus his hands were steady until the sun set. So Joshua overwhelmed Amalek and his people with the edge of the sword (Ex. 17:8-13).

Notice that Moses was the leader, but Joshua was doing the fighting. Even with Moses' limited role in the battle that day, he needed help. Granted, getting Mo a rock stool and propping his arms up does not show up on anybody's list of spiritual gifts, but that was what God led them to do. We really don't know what

Jesus was a walking, talking example of the who? in Bible study!

God was teaching Moses and the people that day. Maybe He was showing them that prophets, pastors, or even youth ministers need help, even if it is just holding their arms up.

In the very next chapter, Moses' father-in-law, Jethro, noticed something about Moses' leadership:

And it came about the next day that Moses sat to judge the people, and the people stood about Moses from the morning until the evening. Now when Moses' father-in-law saw all that he was doing for the people, he said, "What is this thing that you are doing for the people? Why do you alone sit as judge and all the people stand about you from morning until evening?" And Moses said to his father-in-law, "Because the people come to me to inquire of God. "When they have a dispute, it comes to me, and I judge between a man and his neighbor, and make known the statutes of God and His laws."

And Moses' father-in-law said to him, "The thing that you are doing is not good. "You will surely wear out, both yourself and these people who are with you, for the task is too heavy for you; you cannot do it alone. "Now listen to me: I shall give you counsel, and God be with you. You be the people's representative before God, and you bring the disputes to God, then teach them the statutes and the laws, and make known to them the way in which they are to walk, and the work they are to do.

"Furthermore, you shall select out of all the people able men who fear God, men of truth, those who hate dishonest gain; and you shall place these over them, as leaders of thousands, of hundreds, of fifties and of tens. "And let them judge the people at all times; and let it be that every major dispute they will bring to you, but every minor dispute they themselves will judge. So it will be easier for you, and they will bear the burden with you. "If you do this thing and God so commands you, then you will be able to endure, and all these people also will go to their place in peace."

So Moses listened to his father-in-law, and did all that he had said. And Moses chose able men out of all Israel, and made them heads over the people, leaders of thousands, of hundreds, of fifties and of tens. And they judged the people at all times; the difficult dispute they would bring to Moses, but every minor dispute they themselves would judge (Ex.18:13-26).

Moses needed help, and Jethro was wise enough to see what was going on. Moses was getting burned out because he heard whiny disputes all day. The people were getting worn out because they had to wait in line all day. Jethro suggested something very profound. What if Moses (or the minister of youth or the pastor, or anyone else in charge of youth ministry) studied the Scripture to see what God had in mind for the people? Then, what if the leader trained some other people to handle smaller facets of the work? Then, what if the people knew they had someone they could call to answer questions about the Bible or about life?

It sounds strangely like the way we do Sunday School, doesn't it? Caring adults agree to shepherd small groups of teenagers so that youth ministers and pastors and volunteer youth coordinators can deal with big-picture problems. Thank you for being a crucial *who?* in youth ministry! In chapter 6, we will explore more of the *who?* that you bring to the class as a leader. You will have a chance to give some thought to your particular way of processing information as a teacher.

WHO ARE THESE KIDS?

In the old movie, "Butch Cassidy and the Sundance Kid," Paul Newman and Robert Redford were being pursued by a posse of extremely professional lawmen hired by the Pinkertons. The outlaws had never been chased by anyone that good before. The question they continually asked as they looked over their shoulders to see if the posse was gaining ground was, "Who are these guys?"

We are called to minister in a culture of teenagers that can be scary. In the remainder of this chapter, let's look deeper into the *who?* of our ministry. Who is involved in the Bible teaching ministry with youth? We have to consider youth, friends of youth, families of youth, youth workers, families of youth workers, even the youth minister. Keep in mind all of the personalities that Jesus dealt with in Luke 9-10! We cannot ever forget the most important *Who?* in the equation: the Holy Spirit will assist us as well.

Remember the subject is preparation. *How do we prepare for these youth?* How do we prepare for the unexpected guests who show up at Bible study because they spent the night with one of our kids? Let's look at this systematically. First we'll review some things that are common to most all youth. Then we'll look at some cultural patterns or groups that may make your ministry interesting. Finally, I want to briefly contextualize the *who?* of youth ministry in the family situations that you will likely encounter. Here are a few more questions to get you thinking:

- Who have we taught?
- Who are we teaching?
- Who will we teach?

IT'S JUST PART OF PUBERTY

The collection of *who?* in every youth ministry and community is made up of individual adolescents. The physical development of adolescence is called "puberty." Puberty and adolescence are not the same thing—*puberty* is the beginning of the rapid physical changes that signal the beginning of adolescence; *adolescence* is the term that describes the "between time" after puberty but before adult responsibility. Depending upon the age group of the students with whom you work, these physical changes vary. Mental changes are also taking place. Teenagers are moving toward an ability to deal with abstract thought (more about that later). They are increasingly able to deal with concepts and possibilities. They are moving toward stability (relatively!) from an emotional standpoint. Their social world is expanding, sometimes with a movement away from family to peers. Finally, youth are developing spiritually. Sometimes we overlook the fact that the development that is apparent in other areas of an adolescent's life is active in their faith as well.

For a summary, (probably more of a reminder to most of you!) of some of the normal and predictable changes that occur in adolescence, see pages 20-21 in *Youth Sunday School for A New Century* by Chuck Gartman and Richard Barnes. Remember that the physical changes experienced by teenagers are complex. As leaders we need to learn about how they develop, not only physically, but intellectually, emotionally, socially and spiritually.

HELLO, THIS IS THE BRAIN SPEAKING!

There is new evidence that the teen brain is actually different from other brains. (Let me wait for the laughter to die down.) Now, this gem of research is something you have suspected for some time, but let me confirm that

- yes, they all have brains;
- and yes, those brains are operating differently than the brains of children or adults.

Magnetic resonance imaging has shown that the teen brain is immature. I do not mean immature in a childish behavior sort of way, but that the neural circuits are not fully in place until the person is in his or her early 20's. Different parts of the brain develop according to a different timetable, just like the rest of the body during puberty. The brain has not finished forming the ability to make wise judgments, and mediate emotions. Also "under construction" is the refinement of

WHO
have we
taught?

WHO
are we
teaching?

WHO
will we teach?

HOW
do we prepare
for these youth?

"Too much too soon" for a sixth grader often results in boredom.

motor and mental abilities. Shannon Brownlee, author of an article in *The U.S. News and World Report* on the teen brain made an important observation for adults who work closely in the lives of youth:

". . . it might be unreasonable to expect young teenagers to organize multiple tasks or grasp abstract ideas. And these still developing neural links leave a teenager vulnerable: Depression in adolescence may set up circuits in the brain that will make it much harder to treat the illness later in life . . . . But these changes aren't all for the worse. The brain's capacity for growth through adolescence may also indicate that even troubled teenagers can still learn restraint, judgment, and empathy."[3]

Whether physical, mental, social, emotional, or spiritual, the precious youth in our care are works in progress. When you consider all of the influences (more on influence in a moment) in the lives of our teenagers, you realize how vital your role is. You partner with the Holy Spirit in the shaping of these developing creatures. Understanding the *who?* is half the fun!

THE MYSTERY OF THE WHO? IN SIXTH GRADE

One final developmental loose end is the response to the question, "What do I do with 6th Graders?" If you have teenagers in your home, you already know what I am about to say. Fact: teenagers do not all develop on the same timeline. In relationship to peers, some reach puberty earlier than others. Fact: girls mature, on the average, two years before boys. If you add up these two facts and do a little deduction, you come to the conclusion that you could possibly have a class of sixth graders with a wide developmental gap. If you have in your class a late maturing boy and an early maturing girl, they can be (be patient with me while I do the math) four years apart developmentally, even if they share the same birthday!

This dilemma is multiplied many times over if you group sixth graders with seventh and eighth graders in a middle school grouping. The gap is magnified even farther if you include sixth graders with the entire youth group. Some of you who are reading this book have placed sixth graders in your Youth Division because of a small enrollment or because of a middle school arrangement (grades 6-8 in one school) in your public or private schools. May I remind you of a few general principles?

- No matter where sixth graders are located in a school system, they will still learn content on a sixth-grade level.
- Because sixth graders think mostly in concrete terms, they need materials and methods that do not require them to think in abstract terms (at least not all the time).
- Although some sixth graders have matured physically, emotional maturity often lags behind. A sixth-grade girl in a tenth-grade body may be attractive to eleventh-grade boys. This can be a father's nightmare.
- While sixth graders may be only two years behind eighth graders chronologically, some late maturers are as much as five years behind developmentally. Loss of self-esteem may be the price paid when a child cannot succeed at the skill levels of older kids.
- Most sixth graders are not ready to interact socially with seventh through twelfth graders. When they are grouped with the junior high and high schoolers, the older youth may drop out, rather than cope with the immaturity of sixth graders.
- "Too much too soon" for a sixth grader often results in boredom. Involvement in all youth activities at an early age may lead to burnout and dropout by the time they reach eleventh and twelfth grade.

OK, it's time to put on our investigative reporter hats again and ask, "So what?" If we will keep these developmental characteristics of individual youth in mind as we prepare ourselves and the ministry environment, we may avoid some of the typical difficulties that accompany teaching teenagers. Now let's look at the youth who may (or may not) be in your class.

WHATEVER HAPPENED TO WALLY AND "THE BEAVE"?

Occasionally, it is said of me that I have "an amazing grasp for the obvious." It therefore would not stun you for me to observe that the youth culture has changed a bit in the last few years. The section preceding this one was intended to remind us that some things remain relatively constant with individual teenagers. This section is to remind us that very little remains constant in the *culture* in which those individuals live and breathe. Because we have limited space here, I want to hit only a few of the highlights of this rapidly changing landscape.

Ward and June Cleaver raised Wally and Beaver in a world that had very little variety. There were no black or brown faces on "Leave it to Beaver"—only white ones. Everyone had pretty much the same accent, and the definition of "bad" was Eddie Haskell, not teenagers who commit multiple homicide in the school library.

Culture relates to ideas, feelings, and values. The *cognitive* dimension of culture means that a culture shares ideas, tools, language, educational systems, and basic assumptions about the nature of the world. The *affective* dimension of culture has to do with the feelings people have. The affective domain in culture involves what persons in a culture consider to be attractive, or tasteful, fashionable, or even enjoyable. The youth culture is extremely emotional (a culture without emotions—where everything is functional or utilitarian, would be drab and uniform.)

A third aspect of culture and cultures is the evaluative dimension. Every culture has a system of valuing or judging what is considered moral or immoral, ethical or unethical, even legal or illegal. Some occupations or cliques are ranked as more or less acceptable than others. Every culture has a code of conduct with the ultimate violations of the code as the taboos of the particular culture. For Christians, the code of conduct is rooted in Scripture, with the ultimate evaluative test as that which pleases or honors God.

Investigative reporters, as you read this, you are already shifting into "so what?" mode, so make this leap with me. Research has shown that youth as a whole are disconnecting from the evaluative systems of the Christian faith. Two-thirds of adolescents today believe there is no such thing as absolute truth (that which is true for all situations). The concept of spiritual transformation is crucial in light of this dynamic. If participation in youth ministry or in Youth Sunday School only produces knowledge (cognitive dimension) or even guilt (affective dimension), it has fallen short of the mark. The goal of studying the Scripture is to see lives changed (evaluative dimension). It's all about change.

INTRODUCTION TO YOUTH CULTURE

The study of youth culture is an exhaustive task. As we investigate the *who?* of who is or isn't going to be in our classes, we need to be sure to keep perspective. The extremes in our culture cry out for attention, yet the majority of the youth in our youth groups are between the extremes. A few of the reasons we look at the culture as a whole:
- It is wise to know what's going on in the culture (1 Chron. 12:32).
- We need to stay in perspective (Jer. 9:23-24).
- Let's learn the culture so that we can minister in it without being of it.

It would be arrogant of me to presume to do an adequate job here of covering the whole picture. Other folks have made it their life's work to study the adolescent culture. Among them are two number-crunching trend readers, George Barna and George Gallup. Their research organizations have helped us understand trends in youth culture as viewed through the lens of statistics. (Check out www.barna.org and www.Gallup.org.) Walt Mueller has researched the youth culture by interviewing youth, studying them, and writing about them. Look with me at a few of the significant aspects of this culture.

• There are a lot of teenagers—about 22 million in America (13-19 year olds with more on the way! Government population statistics show that there are 35,654 million 5-13 year-olds waiting to become teenagers![4]

• They are ripe for a discipleship relationship with Christ. Several studies over the years have shown that fewer than 1 in 10 persons come to know Jesus as Savior after their 19th birthday. Barna's research in November 1999, indicates that the most likely group to receive Christ is the 4-13 age group. This new data challenges the widely-held belief that the teenage years are the best years for evangelistic activity. However, I respectfully disagree with Barna's conclusions. The ability of the teenage mind to comprehend sin, heaven, and hell make it a critical time to lock into a lifetime commitment to Jesus. The foundational discipleship in Sunday School is critical for the processing of the decision to follow Jesus.

• They energize the church. Statistics aren't needed to comment on the tremendous energy boost that teenagers give any worship service, mission project, or church workday.

• They can draw parents. Barna's study pointed out that children and adolescents are most impacted with the gospel by family members, peers, and their youth group (e.g. Sunday School, mid-week faith-based youth activities). The converse can be true. When parents see the effects of transformational discipleship in the life of their teenager, the appeal to find out about the change agent leads to some interesting conversations.

THE "ISMS" OF YOUTH CULTURE

Many terms have been used to describe the youth culture of today. Grouped under a broad heading called "postmodernism," we find other terms that have been used to try to get a handle on youth and the world they live in. Individualism has "I need no one" as its motto. "We are separate beings; we are not connected;" and "I must express myself." Pluralism is the idea that life is multiple choice. Values may come from any number of religions or denominations. No religion is dominant or absolute. Relativism is at the heart of moral relativism. What is true for you is not necessarily true (or right) for me. Everything is "OK" except intolerance. Naturalism is another term for agnosticism or even atheism, meaning that everything can be explained within the context of "natural" forces. Naturalism is prevalent among educational systems that our teenagers attend.

This is the millennial generation, sandwiched between the baby busters and the "Y2Kers" (my term). They are an optimistic bunch. They have never known war that wasn't fought from the air like a video game. The economy has been healthy in their lifetime. They are able to achieve academically (although many of them are not doing so). Their choices are virtually unlimited from 200 cable television channels to nearly-instantaneous Internet surfing that takes them anywhere in the world.

They are not without problems. Mueller points out their families are changing, media is more of an influence than ever, moral relativism has confused their decision making and a prevailing sense of hopelessness is fairly common in the culture. In spite of the contradiction between the optimism and the hopelessness, Mueller commented on the "generation gap" that exists between these teenagers and adults who parent and work with them:

"I'm convinced this is a gap nobody wants. If we take the time to understand and really know kids, then we'll be able to cross into their culture, close the gap, and give them the biblical answers and positive direction they so desperately need. Today's children and teens will only be a 'lost generation' if we forsake our God-given responsibility to love and lead." [5]

CROSS-CULTURAL MINISTRY

I have seen very few multi-cultural youth ministries. Increasingly, multiracial ministry is evident, but only a few of these have truly crossed cultural lines. Race is a concept used to identify large groups of people who share hereditary characteristics. Culture has to do with ways of behavior, socioeconomics, values and so forth (see above). Some people have even predicted that class will replace race as the next great barrier in youth group unity. Some writers identify the cross-cultural nature of Jesus' ministry. For example, Jesus crossed cultural lines to minister to:

- The woman at the well (John 4:3-30).
- The Roman centurion and Samaritan leper (Luke 7:1-10,11-19).
- The world via the Great Commission (Matt. 28:19)

Some church folks say that we should just minister to the people who are like us, or who come to us. It is understandable that it is difficult to get used to change and to a world that is less and less alike each day. We live in a culturally pluralistic society. Youth workers who are committed to loving all kinds of youth will learn an appreciation for and acceptance of the contributions and enrichment that come with cultural diversity. To illustrate this, let me quote a story from *Connected, Committed and a Little Bit Crazy*:

The Techwood Baptist Mission was a mission sponsored by the church I served in Atlanta. They did not have their own baptistry, so when baptism was in the order of worship, the came to our church (the "mother church"). The Techwood congregation was from inner city Atlanta, and we had virtually nothing in common socially, economically, historically, or culturally. Yet, when they cheered and clapped and raised their hands in celebration when one of their new believers passed through the waters of baptism, I was caught offguard. At first, I thought, "Don't they know they are disrupting the dignity and reverence of the moment?" Then, I thought, *Allen, if thousands of angels are rejoicing, who am I to sit on my hands?*

In this I experienced the heart of multi-cultural ministry. The differences in background and culture are lost in the common denominators of faith, hope, and love. I cannot watch baptism with a unicultural perspective any longer. Now I want to stand up and cheer!

LEARNING ABOUT YOUTH CULTURE

It is difficult to have an effective relationship with anyone if you have no idea what their world is like. The world of teenagers includes their family, friends, school, community, music, movies, television, fashion, life issues—whew! What if you as a youth leader want to find out more about youth culture? Talk to them. You can start with your own youth group. Find out the answers to questions like:

- What are the defining moments in their lives (those "I remember where I was when this happened" kind of things?
- What are their weekly life-changing experiences?
- Where do youth spend their free time?

- How is their family? Ask them to describe the health of parent or sibling relationships.
- What types of electronic media do they prefer?
- How much are they aware of national or global events and how are those events shaping their lives?
- How do they communicate (with friends, family, God)? What methods of communication do they use?
- Ask them to describe their religion (don't give them any more clues!).
- Who are their heroes?
- What are their dreams?
- What are their fears?
- What do they want to be doing in five years?

SPECIAL NEEDS YOUTH

One of the most difficult aspects of youth ministry involves youth who are different from the average teens in church. These youth have needs that present challenges greater than those of other youth and require customized attention.

A recent report issued by OSEP to Congress states that over the past few years, the number of school-age students with disabilities served by IDEA (Individuals with Disabilities Education Act) has increased at a higher rate than the general school enrollment. The report states that the number of students ages 12-17 with disabilities increased 30.7 percent and the largest single category is learning disabilities, with 62.3 percent of students in that age group.

It's hard to provide special assistance for those teenagers, yet it sometimes seems impossible to include them. The issue revolves around whether or not to include youth with special needs in the general youth programs of the church. Nationally there has been gradual progress in serving larger percentages of students with disabilities in regular class environments and regular schools (inclusion) and in 1995-96, more than 95 percent of students with disabilities ages 6-21 attended schools with their nondisabled peers.[6]

The term *Special Education* covers a broad spectrum, but LifeWay focuses on six primary areas. The types of special needs encountered in youth ministries usually can be described within these categories:

Mental Handicap.—A condition that causes a person's intellectual and social development to be much lower than most other persons of the same age. Most cases of mental disability are genetic, prenatal or birth-trauma related. Many children, however, become disabled due to lack of educational opportunities, poor nutrition, and poverty.

Visual Impairment.—Most visually impaired students have vision that is between 20/70 and 20/200; they are sometimes called low vision students. (20/200 means that a person can see at 20 feet what persons with normal eyesight can see at 200 feet.) Those with vision 20/200 or worse are classified as blind, but most have some vision, even though it is limited. The common causes of visual disabilities among youth are prenatal influences (heredity), injuries, poisoning, tumors, and infectious diseases.

Learning Disability.—There is much controversy over the true definition of a learning disability; different professionals use different definitions. For our purposes, and in order to keep it somewhat simple, we will describe a person with a learning disability as one with normal or higher intelligence who has problems in understanding language; this may result in low levels of ability in listening, thinking, talking, reading, writing, spelling, math, or memory. The most common examples that youth workers encounter are youth with ADD (Attention Deficit Disorder) or ADHD (Attention Deficit Hyperactivity Disorder). A student can have ADHD or ADD and not have a learning disability according to most definitions, but it is very common to see students with both. These students are characterized by a short attention span, impulsiveness, distractibility, poor listening skills, and disruptiveness.

Gifted.—Gifted youth exhibit significantly above-average intelligence or talents that require special attention to nurture and develop. Giftedness can be found in general academics, specific disciplines (reading, math, languages, writing), talents in music or art, leadership skills, or interpersonal skills.

Physical Disability.—A permanent condition that hinders a person's ability to carry out the activities of daily living because of a limited ability to move. Causes of physical disabilities may include:

- spina bifida—a failure of the spinal column to close during fetal development, creating open defects in the spinal canal;
- cerebral palsy—a nonprogressive disorder of movement or posture that occurs before, during, or immediately after birth or in early childhood and is caused by brain damage or dysfunction;
- muscular dystrophy—a breaking down of muscle cells that are replaced by fat and fibrous tissue;
- arthritis—an inflammation of joints or other parts of the body;
- traumatic injury—paraplegia (paralysis of the legs) and quadriplegic (paralysis of arms and legs)
- amputations—surgical loss of arms and/or legs

Deaf/Hearing Impairment.—Some youth have difficulty hearing and understanding or total inability to hear spoken words or music. They are generally adept at compensation for their hearing loss through signing and/or lip reading.

Other.—There are other areas considered by the public school system to be Special Education areas that may be exhibited by teens in Sunday School. Among them are autism, behavioral disorders, speech impairments, and traumatic brain injuries.

Often, we youth workers are uninformed about the specific type of disability a youth in our class or youth group has. The preceding situations may not be present in your group of youth; but when they are, frustration can result on the part of youth workers who feel inadequate to deal with these special needs youth. Adults who are committed to special needs teenagers will become educated about the types of disabilities involved and they will seek creative ways to teach and minister to those youth.

In most cases in Youth Sunday School, it is recommended to mainstream teenagers with disabilities. Adult workers with youth should keep an eye out to assist in the inclusion of special needs youth. Accessibility to Youth Sunday School areas should be confirmed. Sometimes classmates can provide assistance using the concept of "peer tutoring." Adaptation of teaching plans may be necessary. For youth who are hearing impaired, plan more visual activities or arrange seating so the youth can see your lips. Be sensitive to youth who may have visual impairment with regard to handouts or written activities. A little extra time spent on planning your Sunday morning Bible study can bring great rewards as you meet the needs of these special youth.

A BRIEF WORD ABOUT FAMILIES

One of the principles that you will study in a few chapters is that Sunday School is a place where families are strengthened. Sunday School affirms that the home is the center of biblical guidance. One of the strategic principles in 21st century Sunday School is the principle of family responsibility.[7] Yet, we must be intentional about our understanding that a major *who?* of doing youth ministry is the family. We have to do a better job of partnering with families in the 21st century. That may mean that we take a critical look at some of the things we do that actually hurt families. Chap Clark and Pam Erwin authored a chapter in *New Directions for Youth Ministry* in which they offered eight mistakes we often make concerning youth ministry planning and families:[8]

- Not considering family time and needs when scheduling youth events
- Assuming the role of parents
- Making parents look bad
- Not keeping parents informed
- Not encouraging or offering support for families
- Undermining parents' judgment or authority
- Not including families in youth events
- Failing to connect teenagers with the extended church family

When we think through the who? of preparing to teach the Bible, we can get information overload in a hurry. As you *continue* in your role as investigative reporter, don't be discouraged by the flood of ideas. Keep in mind that relationships are what makes Sunday School (or for that matter, youth ministry) work. When you discover the who? you are ready to move on to the what? and the how?

Endnotes

[1] "Apostles" from *Nelson's Illustrated Bible Dictionary*, Copyright © 1986, Thomas Nelson Publishers

[2] Adapted from the *Life Application Bible*, published by Tyndale House Publishers.

[3] "Inside the Teen Brain" by Shannon Brownlee, U.S. News and World Report, August 8, 1999. Accessed at http://www.usnews.com, September 1, 19994

[4] http://www.census.gov/population/estimates/nation/ accessed 12/8/99.

[5] Walt Mueller, quoted on the CPYU Web site www.cpyu.org, accessed 12/8/99.

[6] Twentieth Annual Report to Congress on the Implementation of the Individuals with Disabilities Act, 1998, downloaded from the internet December 8, 1999.

[7] Chuck Gartman and Richard Barnes, *Youth Sunday School for A New Century*, Nashville: LifeWay, 1998,8.

[8] Chap Clark and Pamela Erwin, "Reconstructing Family Life," in *New Directions for Youth Ministry*: Loveland, CO, Group Publishing, 1998, 49-52.

sunday school affirms that the home is the center of biblical guidance.

CHAPTER 3

WHAT DOES IT MEAN TO TEACH YOUTH?

The new definition for Sunday School for a New Century includes the dual objectives of leading people to faith in the Lord Jesus Christ and building Great Commission Christians through Bible study groups. Let's look more closely at what it means to *teach youth the Bible* and identify some biblical principles we can apply to getting prepared to teach.

Teaching is one of three strategies in Matthew 28:18-20 for accomplishing the one Great Commission to make disciples. Three words modify *make disciples*. The first word identifies the first strategy: *Go*—that is, get out of the routine of your daily life to go where youth are. Also, *go* can mean "as you go" through your daily relationships and responsibilities, seizing everyday opportunities to share the gospel, minister, and teach.

The second phrase, *baptizing them in the name of the Father, the Son and of the Holy Spirit*, speaks of publicly professing faith in Christ. By obeying Christ in baptism, youth symbolize their faith in Jesus' death and resurrection and picture their transformation of dying to an old life and being raised to new life in Christ. Strategically, Great Commission teachers intentionally seek to lead youth to salvation through faith in Christ and then assimilate them into the church.

To focus on the teaching strategy, take a careful look at the third phrase, *teaching them to obey everything I have commanded you*. Here, Jesus identified both the goal and the scope of Great Commission teaching. Jesus gave us content to teach— "everything I have commanded you." There's no part of the Bible that youth should not study. Sunday School champions the absolute truth and authority of the Word of God and calls youth to integrate a biblical worldview into their minds, hearts, and lives through ongoing systematic Bible study.

We are not to stop at teaching Bible content. We are to teach youth to obey what Jesus commanded. God gave us His Word not just to inform us but to transform us. The goal of Bible study is transformed lives that exhibit love for God and others.[1] Jesus called for transformation in the way people think, feel, and act—their minds, emotions, and wills. Such lives glorify God by being Christlike in nature.[2]

Picking up on what we saw in Jesus' ministry in Luke 9:2,11, our teaching ministry must be driven by a vision for God's kingdom—for the reign and rule of Christ in every heart. When Jesus set His heart toward Jerusalem in Luke 9:51, He set His life on course for the cross. Like Jesus, we who teach youth must set our course on the kingdom mission of teaching youth for spiritual transformation.

TEACHING YOUTH FOR SPIRITUAL TRANSFORMATION

Although the Holy Spirit gives the spiritual gift of teaching to individuals within a church, all believers are called to teach.[3] Teaching youth the Bible means leading them to interact with God's Word in a ministry environment that is conducive to the Holy Spirit's work of spiritual transformation.

Spiritual transformation is God's work of changing a believer into the likeness of Jesus by creating a new identity in Christ and by empowering a lifelong relationship of love, trust, and obedience to glorify God.

Twenty-first century teachers recognize that teaching does not stop when the session ends; it is a seven-day-a-week strategy. Teaching youth for spiritual transformation starts in the leader's heart before the session, introduces youth to transforming truth during the session, and continues teaching and learning after the session. Great Commission teaching has:
- Christ as the authority ("all authority").
- People as the focus ("them").
- Obedience as the goal ("to obey").
- God's Word as the content ("everything I have commanded you").
- Christ's presence as the power ("I am with you always").

BIBLICAL INSTRUCTION

The concept of instruction reflects the heartbeat of the Bible. The Bible is the source book for instruction (2 Tim. 3:16). To live out a biblical worldview in a pluralistic, secular culture, every believer must understand the Bible and what it means to live according to the rule of God in His kingdom.

 In the Old Testament, the Lord informed Moses that He would give him the Ten Commandments for the people's "instruction" (Ex. 24:12). Parents became primarily responsible for instructing their children in the ways of God (Deut. 6:4-9). In its most primitive form the Hebrew word for *instruction* means *to throw* or *to shoot*. Included is a sense of directionality.

 In the New Testament, the Greek word for *training* in 2 Timothy 3:16 and Ephesians 6:4 means a blend of instruction, discipline, and personal guidance. Generally, *instruction* means to train or direct learners to build their lives upon a structure of authoritative precepts or truths. Such instruction is best when characterized by a systematic plan and a call to conform to truth.

 Instruction has "edge" to it, in that those who teach have a sense of urgency and passion. Instructors typically deal with issues that change people's lives and warn of the consequences of failing to follow the directives. Flight instructors teach pilots with intensity because not only is the life of the pilot at stake, but also the lives of the pilot's passengers are on the line. Instruction in spiritual matters also includes intensity and passion, for the eternal welfare of people is at stake. Bible teachers intentionally lead participants to the spiritual "fork in the road" that demands decision. Bible teachers are like signposts directing travelers.

 Under the direction of the Holy Spirit, instruction for spiritual transformation includes instruction by godly, loving parents who by word and example guide their children to integrate the Scriptures into their lives; instruction by authentic Christian teachers who model the Christian way of life; and the instruction from holy Scripture as the absolute authority and truth to guide all of life.

 In the larger context of Christ's ministry, the major motivation for such a teaching ministry is obeying the Great Commandment to love God and love others as one's self (Matt. 22:37-40). Paul himself described his motivation as being compelled by God's love (2 Cor. 5:14).

PREPARATION—BOTH PRACTICAL AND BIBLICAL

Human beings tend to be in constant motion. We are always doing something, thinking about doing something, or preparing to do something. Consider preparations teenagers make, for example. When was the last time you heard a middle school band get ready for a concert by tuning its instruments? (How could you forget?) How about a high school baseball player getting ready for his turn at bat in the on-deck circle? (And that stance in the batter's box as he prepares for the pitch!) Or how long a teenaged girl spends in the bathroom getting ready to go somewhere? (Actually, teenage boys typically take longer.) Preparation is a part of everyday life.

 Since we spend time preparing for a typical day's activities, certainly we should prepare to teach youth the Word of God. Preparation is not only practical; it's biblical. The apostle Paul addressed preparation when he wrote to Timothy in 2 Timothy 2:15:

Do your best to present yourself to God as one approved, a workman who does not need to be ashamed and who correctly handles the word of truth.

Bible teachers are like signposts directing travelers.

Note these key elements in Paul's directive:

• *Do your best to present yourself.*—Paul began not with Timothy's teaching methods but with Timothy's personal life. The language here is one of surrender and sacrifice—similar to what Paul wrote in Romans 12:1-2 to present the body as a "living sacrifice." Transformational teaching starts with teachers who are "transformed by the renewing of the mind."

• *To God.*—Only the Lord can bring about spiritual transformation. As God transforms us—the teachers—we assume a prophetic ministry by listening to God's voice, discerning His message, integrating the message into our lives, and speaking His truth in love through His church to the nations.

• *Does not need to be ashamed.*—This clause speaks to the character of the teacher and the power of the gospel. As leaders, we should live based on who we are in Christ—saints (Eph. 1:1), forgiven of our sins (Eph. 1:7), and gifted to build up the body of Christ as we each do our part (Eph. 4:7,16). At the same time, no youth leader should ever be ashamed of the gospel, for the good news of Christ is "the power of God for the salvation of everyone who believes" (Rom. 1:16).

• *Who correctly handles the word of truth.*—Teachers must be competent in handling the Word of God. We must not deceive youth or distort God's Word, but set forth the truth plainly, as Paul wrote in 2 Corinthians 4:2. Youth teachers must practice sound principles of biblical interpretation. We'll examine these principles in the next chapter.

Obviously, preparation takes place before the session. The Holy Spirit can surely give you the words to say on the spur of the moment (Matt. 10:19-20). At the same time, He will also work before the session to speak to you about your own walk with Him and then help you develop a plan for how to teach youth God's Word. Effective Sunday School teachers do not simply prepare lessons; they prepare themselves! Youth will remember your character as the leader much longer than the content of your lessons (Phil. 4:9). The first essential for all effective Sunday School leaders is to be prepared. If nothing else, preparation is a matter of obedience to 2 Timothy 2:15.

TEACHING TO SPIRITUALLY TRANSFORM

What guidelines should we keep in mind as we prepare to teach? While some of the following seem self-evident, they are profoundly transformational for those who teach.

• Use the Bible
• Depend on the Holy Spirit
• Teach God's Word in and Through the Family
• Magnify Relationships with the Learners, Wherever You Gather Them
• Accept Accountability as the Teacher
• Lead Learners to be Accountable
• Engage in Evaluation and Reflection

For more explanation of these guidelines, see *Teaching the Jesus Way: Building a Transformational Teaching Ministry*, by Jay Johnston and Ronald K. Brown.

Endnotes

[1]Matthew 22:37-40; 1 Timothy 1:5.

[2]Psalm 119:1-16,105-112; Romans 12:1-2; 2 Corinthians 3:18; Colossians 3:16-17.

[3]Matthew 28:19-20; Acts 15:35; Ephesians 4:11-13; Colossians 3:16; 2 Timothy 2:2.

CHAPTER 4

How Do We Prepare

TO TEACH YOUTH GOD'S WORD?

Not too long ago, I had the pleasure of enlisting Rick to be a new teacher for the High School Sunday School Department at our church. I thought to myself, *Rick is going to ask me, "What do you expect of me?"* I knew that one commitment I desired from all of our department leaders is to participate in our department leadership meetings. Then it dawned on me: Why not use the three easy-to-remember essentials of teaching for spiritual transformation—*prepare, encounter,* and *continue*—to outline to Rick what I expected of him?

Simply stated, there are three essentials for Bible teaching that lead to spiritual transformation:

- Before the teaching session, *prepare* the ministry environment for spiritual transformation.
- During the session, guide youth toward spiritual transformation through an *encounter* with God's Word in a Bible study group.
- After the session, *continue* to guide youth toward spiritual transformation in daily living and family relationships.

Beginning in the fall of 2000 you will find in all LifeWay Sunday School for A New Century leader guides a common format with three headings: *Prepare, Encounter,* and *Continue.* These three concepts take teaching God's Word to a new level—from a 60-minute one-day-per-week event to a seven-day-a-week strategy!

Wait a minute! I didn't sign up for a seven-day-a-week strategy! I have a full-time job and obligations! I can't do a seven-day-a-week volunteer ministry!

Before you turn in your resignation, think of teaching youth in terms of 1-2-3: (1) *prepare,* (2) *encounter,* and (3) *continue.* Plan to be a leader who will *prepare* yourself and your lesson, *encounter* God's Word in a youth Bible study group, and then *continue* to look for ways to teach and love youth after the session. Also, think long-term goals with short-term actions. After all, you will have up to 12 months to teach youth. The lesson begins with the session and continues following the session—for days, weeks, and months, even a lifetime!

In this chapter we'll focus on the first of three essentials for teaching for spiritual transformation: Before the session, *prepare* the ministry environment for spiritual transformation. Preparing begins with choosing sound curriculum.

THE CURRICULUM RACE

When I played high school football, our coach required every football player to participate in at least one event in track and field. What was I to do? I couldn't jump high or far, or pole vault. I wasn't big enough to push the shot put or throw the discus. My only option was to run a race. The sprints and relays were out; the hurdles kept getting in my way. There was only one race left for me—the mile run. I still draw life's lessons from my high school days of running mile-long races.

Essentially, *curriculum* refers to the course, track, or path on which a person runs. Curriculum is similar to running a race toward a finish line, much as the author of Hebrews encouraged his readers in Hebrews 12:1 to "run with perseverance the race marked out for us." Note that the writer called for the race to be run with perseverance and that the race is on a track that is marked out for us. Choosing Bible study curriculum means pursuing the course that the Bible sets for life—Christlikeness, transformation into the image of Christ (Rom. 8:28-29). Sunday School curriculum is the continuous course, process, or system for Bible study groups to use in order to guide unbelievers toward faith in Christ and believers toward Christlikeness through the transforming power of the Holy Spirit. A marathon provides a good analogy, because spiritual transformation is not a short-term experience but a lifelong process. The track chosen for this lifelong process of spiritual transformation should be chosen carefully because it will ultimately affect the learner's worldview.

There are two aspects of curriculum: the curriculum plan and the curriculum resources. The curriculum plan sets the course for what is studied. We'll examine curriculum plans in this chapter. The curriculum resources contain the curriculum plan and set forth how to study it. We'll examine curriculum resources in chapters 6 and 7.

THE RACE TOWARD A BIBLICAL WORLDVIEW

Spiritual transformation begins with conversion at a point in time and continues as a progressive change of worldview that includes a person's values, attitudes, and behavior. As a person grows toward Christlikeness, that individual moves from a lost, secular worldview toward a new, biblical worldview. Sunday School for A New Century curriculum plans set youth on a race toward developing a biblical worldview.[1]

Everyone has assumptions (whether they are conscious of them or not) about what is real, what is true, what is of value, and how to approach life. "Worldview" refers to the collective set of personal convictions people hold and on which they base their actions. A worldview is the lens through which people perceive and understand reality. Stated simply, a worldview is how a person views the world or reality.

A "biblical worldview" describes a worldview that is based upon the Bible and reflects biblical convictions. To view life from a biblical worldview is to view life from God's perspective. As finite creatures, we will never be able to think completely like God. Still, as His people, we can mature and grow toward a worldview that is increasingly consistent with God's worldview. As believers we want to interpret life through the lens of Scripture.

A person's worldview can be defined by how he or she answers certain questions about life. These questions may never be consciously articulated, but how an individual answers these questions captures the essence of his or her worldview. The Sunday School for a New Century biblical worldview model proposes that there are three fundamental life questions for every individual: *Where did I/we come from? How do I/we fit in? and Where am I/we going?* The good news is that there is a personal God who sees, understands, and has in fact created the desire to understand life. Furthermore, this God has spoken in an objective and intelligible manner. He has provided answers to our deepest yearnings:

- *Where did I/we come from?* According to the Bible, Jehovah God created all things with purpose, and He created all people in His image.
- *How do I/we fit in?* The Bible teaches that although everyone has sinned and rebelled against God, He graciously offers forgiveness, restoration, purpose, and community through His Son Jesus Christ.
- *Where am I/we going?* The Scriptures promise that through Christ's salvation, God is present and active both now and forever in those who receive Him.

YOUTH CURRICULUM PLANS

All Sunday School for a New Century curriculum plans have ten common characteristics. The ten characteristics are Biblical Authority, The Kingdom of God, The Biblical Worldview, The Sunday School Strategy, Foundational Evangelism, Foundational Discipleship, Family Responsibility, Spiritual Transformation, Biblical Leadership, and Teach to Transform.

A curriculum plan, or "curriculum map" as some call it, is an orderly arrangement of Bible study content organized so that Bible study leaders can engage learners in the study of God's Word to meet spiritual needs through planned teaching-learning experiences. Well-developed curriculum plans set out to reach specified learning objectives. Such objectives are grouped into a taxonomy, or system and classification of learning goals. (See "Understanding the Curriculum Design and Scope" [Family Bible Study] and the Developmental Life Issues charts for LifeTrak curriculum in the appendix.)

THE FOUR LEGS OF THE CURRICULUM RELAY

Like the relay team with four skilled runners, the curriculum race toward spiritual transformation and a biblical worldview is run best when four principles are put into the race. LifeWay curriculum planners use principles to "map" the dated Family Bible Study plan. If you choose to use *LifeTrak* undated resources to develop your own curriculum plan, you should review these principles as you select which studies to study when.

1. *Comprehensiveness.*—The curriculum plan is comprehensive of all of the Bible (2 Tim. 3:16) and all of youth life issues from grades 7 through 12.

2. *Balance.*—The curriculum plan has a balance of biblical content, Bible study approaches, and life issues. Why not just choose whatever the youth want to study or whatever the "hot topic" is? By following a systematic, comprehensive plan, ongoing Bible study points repeatedly to the fact that the Bible must guide and shape believers' lives. The curriculum plan needs to address head-on where youth are. However, a balanced curriculum plan will not only address the "hot topics" and "felt needs," but will place youth in the race toward mature biblical faith.

3. *Sequence.*—The curriculum plan is properly sequenced so that learners can build on biblical chronology and what they already know. Remember that spiritual transformation toward Christlikeness is life-long. Because curriculum is best

As believers we want to interpret life through the lens of scripture.

viewed from the perspective of a marathon, appropriate repetition of biblical content and life concerns in different ways and at different times strengthens learners, much as a fresh cup of water invigorates a marathon runner. At the same time, "open" Bible study groups will always have new youth joining the curriculum race—new learners who'll need the basics the experienced learners could help teach. Do a quick survey of Jesus' teaching in the Gospels, and you'll discover how frequently He repeated themes—and how slowly His disciples caught on.

4. *Ministry environment.*—Sunday School groups are open groups because they exist not only for those who attend, but also for those who do not come. A good Sunday School curriculum plan reflects an intentional, ongoing open Bible study strategy that is conducive to creating a ministry environment that fosters strong relationships and regularly invites the lost to believe in Christ.

Teaching the Jesus Way: Building a Transformational Teaching Ministry, by Jay Johnston and Ronald K. Brown explains the guidelines you should use to select or develop an ongoing curriculum plan. (See section 5.)

Beginning with the fall of 2000 you will find these curriculum plans available for youth Bible study from LifeWay Christian Resources.

FAMILY BIBLE STUDY

When thinking about the Family Bible Study curriculum plan for youth, keep in mind that Family Bible Study reflects a common curriculum plan designed to achieve the goal of "Building the Family of Faith to Live by God's Truth." This Bible study plan provides a common Bible study theme each week for the five Sunday School age divisions—preschool, children, youth, young adults, and adults—with common Bible passages for all ages as often as suitable. This study plan encourages Bible study at home through "Family Bible Time," a weekly emphasis in the home for parents to guide their children in a discussion of the Bible study theme.

Family Bible Study uses a comprehensive, balanced, and appropriately sequenced study of Bible books, people, doctrine, history, and classic Bible passages. The content is organized around biblical worldview questions (*Where did I/we come from? How do I/we fit in? Where am I/we going?*) and addresses life issues for each age group. In addition to encouraging family responsibility for living God's Word, the common Bible study theme provides opportunity for church leaders to reinforce the biblical truth through music, the pastor's sermon, and mid-week youth worship.

For youth, Family Bible Study offers Bible translation editions in the King James Version and in the New International Version. The Bible text is not printed in leader guides in order to encourage the teacher to teach from his or her own Bible. The Bible text is printed in the learner guides (based on research responses and the benefit of all youth being able to work from a common translation.)

LIFETRAK BIBLE STUDIES FOR YOUNGER YOUTH
AND LIFETRAK BIBLE STUDIES FOR OLDER YOUTH

LifeTrak curriculum is made up of two undated curriculum plans of 13 Bible studies released quarterly. The two Bible study plans cover the message of the Bible and are organized around current developmental life issues distinctive to younger youth and older youth. These issues in turn address the Sunday School for a New Century biblical worldview. (See the LifeTrak charts in the appendix for how the developmental life issues relate to the biblical worldview categories and questions.) LifeTrak is designed for churches that want undated Bible study resources with distinctive curriculum plans for younger and older youth. By using the preceding principles of choosing curriculum, as new volumes are released quarterly you will be able to use LifeTrak to build a curriculum plan distinctive to each grade level. LifeTrak resources are based on the New International Version, but the Bible text is not printed in the leader guide either in "Personal Bible Study" or on the in-class or take-home reproducible pages.

ESSENTIALS FOR LIFE AFTER HIGH SCHOOL

Essentials for Life After High School is a set of 13 undated Bible studies to help high school seniors find biblical guidance to prepare them for life after high school. The 13 studies are: spiritual transformation, personal worship, God's will, priorities, personal impact (evangelism), stewardship, forgiveness, friendship, leadership, intimacy, truth, servanthood, and perseverance. There are also special features on the CrossSeekers program, spiritual heritage, budgeting, servanthood, finding God's will, and identifying spiritual gifts. *Essentials for Life After High School* is designed for churches that want a quarter of Bible studies to help prepare twelfth-grade students for life beyond high school.

Now that you have principles for choosing sound curriculum and curriculum options, you need to prepare the ministry environment by preparing yourself and your lesson before the teaching session.

PREPARE THE MINISTRY ENVIRONMENT

In chapter 3 we defined *teaching youth the Bible* as leading them to interact with God's Word in a ministry environment that is conducive to the Holy Spirit's work of spiritual transformation. The term, *ministry environment*, describes what takes place primarily during the Bible study session. A ministry environment includes the teaching-learning environment, but it is much more. Think of the ministry environment in terms of relationships—among adults and youth, but also relationship with God. Yes, you will want to give attention to the physical setting, especially the walls, chairs, and visuals. But caring relationships among participants are primary. We want to create an environment in which everyone feels welcome and wanted—including the Holy Spirit!

The creation of a ministry environment is directly related to the teacher's own depth of personal spiritual transformation. Teachers should begin with prayer, opening themselves to depend upon the Holy Spirit and to intercede on behalf of relationships and needs within the group. The teacher's ministry of prayer—by name for individual youth and their families—is a powerful daily tool to prepare for transformational teaching.

Teachers then should seek to create an environment for youth to learn biblical truth through establishing personal relationships. When teachers lead their groups to experience fellowship—sharing the common life found only in Christ—not only during the Bible study session; but also throughout other days of the week, they, like Jesus, will be able to communicate biblical truth in a variety of human dilemmas and crises.

Very often, the depth of relationship that the teacher has with the learner affects how well participants are motivated to learn God's Word. When individual youth know they are loved, affirmed, and accepted, they are more likely to be responsive to the teacher's guidance from the authority of God's Word.

What's the best way to prepare yourself and develop plans for such a seven-day-a-week ministry? There are two tried and proven strategies—leadership meetings and personal Bible study. Both build from prayer. To teach like Jesus taught, we must practice prayer in small groups and in private. Leadership meetings are times to pray with others. Personal Bible Study is a time to pray alone.

The creation of a ministry environment is directly related to the teacher's own depth of personal spiritual transformation.

LEADERSHIP MEETINGS

Whether you are the only youth leader or a member of a team of youth leaders in a department, you have three areas of Youth Sunday School ministry to think through before every session. The *Prepare* section of your Youth Sunday School for a New Century leader guide has a section called "Leadership Meeting" where you will find help for you and others to plan for the Bible teaching ministry.

Examine the "Youth Sunday School Plan Sheet" in the appendix as you study each of these three Leadership Meeting areas. You will also find this plan sheet in electronic format on all CD-ROMs in selected Youth Family Bible Study leader packs and in LifeTrak volumes.

Notice the central position given to prayer as you spot the prayer column in the center of the sheet. Now look for the following three headings: *Focus on the Mission, Focus on Relationships,* and *Focus on Bible Study.*

• Focus on the Mission (10 min.)

During this portion of the leadership meeting, the department director guides teachers and other leaders to relate the work of their department and classes to the overall vision and mission of the church and youth ministry. Everyone learns about churchwide and all-youth events and emphases. Also, organizational issues, records, and other administrative concerns are addressed.

• Focus on Relationships (25 min.)

Like Jesus, Great Commission teachers focus on human needs. During this part of the leadership meeting, all leaders look for ways to get involved with youth and prospects during and beyond the Sunday session, especially in evangelism, discipleship, fellowship, ministry, and worship. Discuss the needs of members and prospects and their families and, as appropriate, make plans for responding. Focus especially on ways to involve students in evangelism and ministry. Here's where you could plan fellowship activities and actions to witness to lost youth and assimilate new believers into the department and church.

Churches using the FAITH Sunday School Evangelism Strategy[2] will use this time to review assignments, give reports, and make follow-up assignments.

• Focus on Bible Study (25 min.)

Teaching youth God's Word works best when leaders plan together ways to lead participants to encounter God's Word in a Bible study group. What the department director does in department time should interface with what the teachers do in classes. Such intentional planning maximizes the impact of God's Word on the hearts of individuals and the group as a whole.

Start with evaluating the previous Bible study session. Use this time to preview teaching methods and adapt them. Often another teacher (or student leader, if you enlist them to come) will propose the very idea that will impact the kids the most. Make sure everyone knows what their assignments are for the upcoming study.

Not to be overlooked is the value of this Bible study and prayer time for the adult leaders. Sometimes adults say they do not want to work in Youth Sunday School because their Adult Sunday School class is so meaningful to them. Yet, what a rich Bible study and prayer time the weekly leadership meeting can be just for the adult youth leaders! The leadership meeting is the time to claim Jesus' promise that as we bear fruit, we can ask what we need (John 15:16). Praying for each other as leaders and teachers in a weekly leadership meeting will do wonders to improve the Sunday morning Bible study experience!

PERSONAL BIBLE STUDY

Beyond the Leadership Meeting, you must prepare personally for God to use you to teach His Word. Ask God to speak to you about your own walk with Him. To help you prepare personally, your Sunday School for a New Century leader guide has a section entitled "Personal Bible Study" with interactive Bible study questions to help you, as the teacher, understand and experience God's Word before you teach it.

In the Sunday School for a New Century research project, youth leaders were asked how they would like the material formatted for preparing to teach—all together in one day, or in portions for studying over two to six days. The youth teachers preferred either two-to-three days or all-in-one-day Bible study. In Family Bible Study leader guides, you will find the Scripture passage divided into three major portions that may be studied on three different days. In *LifeTrak Bible Studies for Younger Youth* and *LifeTrak Bible Studies for Older Youth*, you will have the same type of interactive Bible study questions, but they are formatted for all-in-one day preparation. All "Personal Bible Study" sections lead you, the teacher, through the biblical process of instruction that leads to spiritual transformation.

THE SEVEN BIBLE TEACHING ELEMENTS

Remember that spiritual transformation is God's work of changing a believer into the likeness of Jesus by creating a new identity in Christ and by empowering a lifelong relationship of love, trust, and obedience to glorify God. Critical to personal Bible study preparation and developing a lesson plan is understanding how God uses His Word to transform lives. The first calling we have as youth teachers is to let God's Word transform us. Then we can teach from His Word and from the overflow of what God is doing in our lives.[3] Both the Leadership Meeting and Personal Bible Study are times God can use to transform us.

Can we discern from Scripture how God uses His Word to transform lives? Yes, there are seven Bible teaching-learning elements that guide the Bible study process. In this chapter, we will examine the seven elements from the perspective of teachers as they prepare. In later chapters, we will note how the seven elements impact youth both during and after the session.

Teachers should review the seven Bible teaching elements personally before every session. The amount of time a teacher devotes to the seven elements will vary every week. Also, note that the elements are not numbered. Numbering indicates sequence, and while the Holy Spirit generally follows the pattern below, we should never limit how He will work. The important principle is that teachers are experiencing God's work in their lives in these seven areas.

Note that you will find similar questions in the "Prepare" section of the Youth Sunday School Plan Sheet. As you prepare, ask yourself:

- *What authority, power, or rule guides my life related to this passage?*—Acknowledge Authority (control)
- *What did God say in the Scripture to the first readers or hearers?*—Search the Truth (content)
- *What abiding truth(s) for all generations is the Holy Spirit teaching from the Scriptures?*—Discover the Truth (concept)
- *Based on the abiding biblical truth(s), what is God teaching me about thinking, feeling, and living today?*—Personalize the Truth (context)
- *What conflict or crisis of belief is the Holy Spirit bringing about in my heart and life to challenge what I think and value and how I live?*—Struggle with the Truth (conflict)

Q: What if I'm the only youth Bible study leader? As the only adult youth leader in your Youth Sunday School, you may think that a leadership meeting has no relevance for you. Remember, though, every youth leader has the three focus areas of Sunday School ministry to consider before every session: The Mission, Relationships, and Bible Study. If your church uses Family Bible Study, the Bible study theme and often the passage itself is common with other age groups. You could meet with the other age group leaders and share personal insights from the Scriptures and pray for each other. Also, have you thought about occasionally including a key youth as a student leader to plan with you? Or a parent to plan with you, especially related to administrative matters or fellowship, outreach, and ministry? Most importantly, consider enlisting someone to pray with you and for you in your Sunday School ministry. God could use your Youth Sunday School prayer partner to improve your Sunday School without ever stepping into the room!

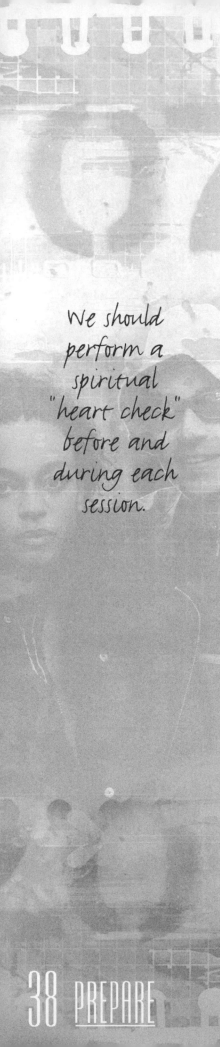

- *How is the Holy Spirit leading me to live and repent—to change my mind, my values, or the way I live—or to resolve the conflict?*—Believe the Truth (conviction)
- *To what extent will I obey the Holy Spirit's leadership in what I think and value and the way I live?*—Obey the Truth (conduct)

Now let's look at these seven Bible teaching elements one at a time.

1. Acknowledge Authority—Control

The first element of teaching God's Word for spiritual transformation is *Acknowledge Authority.* The key word is *control.* A teacher must discern, as far as humanly possible, what authority, power, assumptions, presuppositions, worldview, or rule guides or controls his or her own life in light of the passage being studied. Knowing where we are "coming from" will help us know where we need to make changes in our beliefs, attitudes, or actions. Key questions for discerning the authority in our lives are: *Where is my heart—the final authority in my life—as I approach Bible study? What assumptions—maybe prejudices—do I have about the Bible, this subject, or the people in the Bible study group?*

The element, *Acknowledge Authority,* reminds us that we should perform a spiritual "heart check" before and during each session. Many discipline problems are the result of not discerning where your heart is as the leader and where a teenager's heart is as the learner. Knowing each participant and what controls his or her heart will give you insight in how to guide the person to participate in the Bible study.

Emotions are also vitally important to how much teaching and learning takes place, especially at this point of acknowledging authority. Do all you can to communicate unconditional Christlike love to every youth. Using Jesus as your model, speak the truth in love without compromise. For example, note that Jesus was unwilling to lower standards for those who sought to excuse themselves (Luke 9:58 ff.). At the same time, seek to make the Bible study an experience with lighter moments. For example, try bringing in a log or a two-by-four piece of lumber and holding it up to someone's eye to make the point of Matthew 7:3!

2. Search the Truth—Content

Searching the Scriptures is what most people associate with Bible teaching—reading, examining, and communicating the content of the Bible. And this element of Bible teaching is probably what most teachers have done best. But as a teacher, we must make sure we are interpreting the Scriptures accurately.[4] A great question to ask as we search God's Word is: *What did God say in the Scriptures to the first readers or hearers?* To interpret the Bible accurately, Bible teachers should examine:

- The linguistic factor.—The intended meaning of words and phrases, the relationship of words, and the kind of literature in a particular part of the Scriptures.
- The historical factor.—The historical setting, including the customs of the time, the land and people of the Bible, the language of the Bible, and the archaeology of the Bible.
- The holistic factor.—A focus on understanding the meaning of a particular text in light of how the whole Bible treats the truth or concept.

3. Discover the Truth—Concept

Careful study of what the Bible said to its original readers begs us to ask another question: *What abiding truth(s) for all generations is the Holy Spirit teaching from the Scripture?* Answering this question addresses the third element, *Discover the Truth.* The key word for this element is *concept.* The Bible is much more than a

We should perform a spiritual "heart check" before and during each session.

book of history. It has eternal truths and principles that we can relate to our life questions and issues today. In chapter 8, we will explore how to help youth discover these truths for themselves.

4. *Personalize the Truth—Context*

For *Personalize the Truth*, the key word is *context*. A question to answer is: *Based on the abiding biblical truth(s), what is God teaching me personally about thinking, feeling, and living today?*

In this part of the Bible study process, your understanding of what is going on around you and in you is crucial. Ask yourself, for example, *Given my generational perspective, age, or life stage, what does this spiritual truth mean to me today?* At this point, the Holy Spirit will likely bring to mind how and where the truth impacts your life. This brings us to the next element.

5. *Struggle with the Truth—Conflict*

The fifth element is called *Struggle with the Truth*. The key word is *conflict*. When sinful humans encounter the truth of God's Word, we struggle. Key questions to answer become: *What conflict or crisis of belief is the Holy Spirit bringing about in my heart and life to challenge what I think, value, and how I live? What life questions, problems, issues, trials, or struggles compel me to seek answers and promises in the Bible? What part of my belief system needs to be changed?*

Conflict is the work of the Holy Spirit. Real "application to life" intensifies when we allow ourselves to be honest with how God's Word creates conflict in our hearts, minds, and lives. Even then, we can rejoice when we encounter situations that test our faith (Jas. 1:2-3).

6. *Believe the Truth—Conviction*

The sixth Bible teaching element is *Believe the Truth* and its key word is *conviction*. Key questions to answer are: *How is the Holy Spirit leading me to live and repent—to change my mind, my values, or the way I live—or to resolve the struggle or conflict in my life? What new truth is God leading me to receive and integrate into my life?*

Conviction is the point at which spiritual transformation becomes most intense, for conviction addresses the human will. At this stage—if we are open to the leadership of the Holy Spirit—we are confronted with a change that needs to be made in our lives in order to become more Christlike.

7. *Obey the Truth—Conduct*

Our seventh and final element is *Obey the Truth*. Its key word is *conduct*. The proverbial bottom line question is: *To what extent will I obey the Holy Spirit's leadership in what I think and value and the way I live?*

In the Bible, the word *believe* carries with it more than intellectual assent. In the Bible, believers showed their faith by acting on their faith. In recent years, almost everyone has insisted that Bible study resources "apply the Bible to life." Yet, experienced Bible teachers realize that application means more than merely making a mental connection of biblical truth to a life issue.

Faithfulness to obey God's Word is the ultimate application. "You are slaves of the one whom you obey," wrote the apostle Paul in Romans 6:16 . People who are being spiritually transformed depend upon the Holy Spirit to provide the power for living in obedience to God. Because their old human nature has been crucified with Christ, believers set their minds on Christ who strengthens them (Gal. 2:20; Col. 3:1-17; Phil. 4:13).

When does a believer really understand the meaning of God's Word? Jesus said, "Everyone who hears these words of mine and puts them into practice is like a wise man

Plan from "as youth arrive" to "when they leave."

who built his house on the rock" (Matt. 7:24, NIV). "If you love me," Jesus said, "you will obey what I command" (John 14:15, NIV). Both leaders and learners recognize that people do not complete their Bible study until they obey the Bible in real life.

PUT TOGETHER YOUR PLAN: GO WITH THE FLOW

Twenty-first century Sunday School teachers recognize that there is more teaching to do when the closing prayer ends the Bible study session. Therefore, they plan accordingly. The seven Bible teaching elements can help you think through how to plan the Bible study session and beyond. In chapters 7-8, we'll look at how these seven Bible teaching elements find expression in a good teaching plan for use during and after the session, including how to choose good teaching methods and approaches.

In general, though, keep in mind that every good Bible study session will have a "flow" to it. From the moment youth arrive, choose activities to build relationships and direct their attention to the session's "Biblical Truth" in order to motivate them to want to learn. Every youth comes to a Bible teaching session with an authority—recognized or unrecognized—that controls his or her life (*Acknowledge Authority*). Leaders recognize that they are engaged in spiritual warfare for every person's mind. The beginning of the teaching plan attempts to focus every individual's heart toward learning biblical truth that connects with his or her life.

The next step is to guide students to understand what the passage meant when it was written and its eternal truth(s) for all generations. This next part of the teaching plan engages youth in searching the Scriptures for biblical content and concepts they can understand today (*Search the Truth* and *Discover the Truth*).

Then, help students apply the passage through everyday examples of what youth should "be" and "do." Teaching plans must move youth to *Personalize the Truth*. Inevitably, youth will experience inner conflict as biblical truth intersects with their personal life (*Struggle with the Truth*). Application is not complete until this conflict is resolved by change of belief, attitude, and action as reflected in a lifestyle of love, trust, and obedience that glorifies God (*Believe the Truth* and *Obey the Truth*.) This almost always will come after the session.

A good teacher plans for the whole time that students are in the classroom, from beginning to end. Plan from "as youth arrive" to "when they leave."

Finally, unless you have a remarkable memory, make notes to take with you. You have permission to duplicate the plan sheet in this chapter. You'll find an electronic template of this plan sheet on the CD-ROMs in the selected Family Bible Study leader packs and in LifeTrak; or you can create your own. Try to avoid teaching from your leader guide. Teach from your Bible using the personal notes you have made. Leading youth to use their Bibles begins with us adult leaders using our Bibles. Gather your other resources, pray, and expect to *encounter* the Lord and His young people through studying His Word!

Endnotes

[1] For more information on biblical worldview, see "Biblical Worldview Model" in the appendix.

[2] For general information about FAITH call toll free 1-877-324-8498.

[3] For a Bible study on the seven Bible teaching elements, see Section 6 of *Sunday School for a New Century* by Bill L. Taylor and Louis B. Hanks, Nashville: LifeWay Press, 1999.

[4] For more details on how to interpret the Bible see pages 154-170 in *Christian Scripture: An Evangelical Perspective on Inspiration, Authority and Interpretation* by David S. Dockrey, Nashville: Broadman and Holman, 1995.

CHAPTER 5

WHY ENCOUNTER GOD'S WORD
IN A YOUTH BIBLE STUDY GROUP?

Now that you are familiar with what it means to *Prepare, Encounter,* and *Continue,* and now that you are just about an expert in what it means to *prepare,* we are ready to consider the actual teaching experience. Consider again the newspaper reporter. She has heard about a unique person in her city. She goes out to interview him, and discovers that he is indeed unique. Maybe it is a hobby, an experience, a belief, or an attitude that makes him different, but the story is not in any particular event—the person is the story. Such a story really happened a few years back:

Larry Walters, a 33 year-old truck driver, lived in a cookie-cutter subdivision near the Pacific Ocean (and the Los Angeles International Airport). Every house looked alike, and the routines of the residents were frighteningly similar. Every Saturday, after working all week long, Larry would get a six-pack, sit in the lawn chair in his backyard, and watch his neighbors through the chain link fence (which every yard had).

On July 2, 1982, Walters grew tired of his daily routine. On that Saturday morning, he had an idea that really excited him. He decided to fulfill a lifelong dream and become a pilot! He wanted to go up in a hot air balloon, drift over his neighborhood, and wave to his neighbors. Larry didn't have money for such a balloon, so he bought 45 weather balloons at an army surplus store and a tank of helium. With the help of some friends, he tied the inflated weather balloons to his lawn chair, which was staked to the ground.

After grabbing a bottle of soda, a camera, a portable CB radio, a parachute, and a pellet gun, Larry got in the chair. His plan was to shoot out enough balloons to control the altitude at which he would fly. Well, Larry Walters was a truck driver, not an aeronautical engineer. When his friends cut the ropes, instead of going up 100 feet, he shot up more than 16,000 feet—approximately three miles in the air!

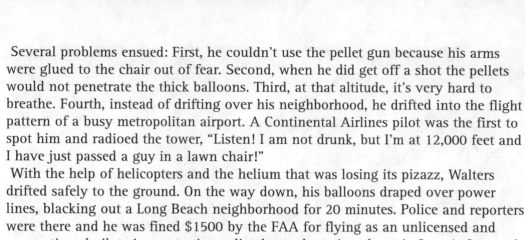

Several problems ensued: First, he couldn't use the pellet gun because his arms were glued to the chair out of fear. Second, when he did get off a shot the pellets would not penetrate the thick balloons. Third, at that altitude, it's very hard to breathe. Fourth, instead of drifting over his neighborhood, he drifted into the flight pattern of a busy metropolitan airport. A Continental Airlines pilot was the first to spot him and radioed the tower, "Listen! I am not drunk, but I'm at 12,000 feet and I have just passed a guy in a lawn chair!"

With the help of helicopters and the helium that was losing its pizazz, Walters drifted safely to the ground. On the way down, his balloons draped over power lines, blacking out a Long Beach neighborhood for 20 minutes. Police and reporters were there and he was fined $1500 by the FAA for flying as an unlicensed and unsanctioned pilot. A reporter immediately stuck a microphone in Larry's face and asked, "Were you scared?" Walters said, "Yep." The reporter asked, "Will you do it again?" Walters said, "Nope." Then the reporter asked, "Why did you do such a thing?" The answer was classic: "There comes a time in your life when you can't just sit there!"[1]

SOMETIMES THE WORD SPEAKS FOR ITSELF—AND WE HELP!

The *why?* of the encounter part of the lesson is to investigate the *why?* of the process, the *why?* of the people who have come, and the *why?* of the teaching-learning experience. The story, however is not necessarily in the teaching event. Like the special interest story that the reporter dug into, the *why?* of the Bible study encounter lies in the:

- motivation of the people who have come;
- giftedness of the adult (or team of adults) who come prepared to guide learning;
- the interaction between the teacher and the learners.

An intriguing aspect of the *why?* of *encounter* is the answer, *because it works!* The preparation of the leader sets the stage for discovery of the truth of God's Word. As the Bible is discovered as Truth by students, a little salt and a little light are sent out into the youth culture. Sometimes we forget that God's Word is pretty powerful on its own. In Isaiah 55:11, the prophet told us, "So shall My word be which goes forth from My mouth; it shall not return to me empty, without accomplishing what I desire, and without succeeding *in the matter* for which I sent it." Psalm 119 is an ongoing testament to what happens when God's word is internalized. For example:

- *How blessed are those whose way is blameless, who walk in the law of the LORD. How blessed are those who observe His testimonies, who seek Him with all their heart. They also do no unrighteousness; they walk in His ways. Thou hast ordained Thy precepts, that we should keep them diligently. Oh that my ways may be established to keep Thy statutes! Then I shall not be ashamed when I look upon all Thy commandments* (Ps 119:1-6).

And perhaps my favorite:

- *How can a young man keep his way pure? By keeping it according to Thy word. With all my heart I have sought Thee; do not let me wander from Thy commandments. Thy word I have treasured in my heart, that I may not sin against Thee* (Ps 119:9-11).

Paul reminds us that the word is "living and active." The biblical writers understood that the supernatural power of God is given to us as we read, study, and memorize His Word. It is power to save, power to transform, and power to live our daily lives. Unfortunately, youth and adults often find that time for Bible study, both personally and in study groups is squeezed out by schedule demands, lack of discipline, or just plain life clutter. The Holy Spirit helps teenagers understand what they are reading. Another aspect of the *why?* of encounter is that protected time for Bible study can keep reminding youth of the importance of biblical literacy.

BACK TO THE WHO? OF PREPARE

Our role as adults is to prepare the environment of *encounter* in such a way that the Word is able to intersect the lives of teenagers. Remember the Ethiopian official who testified as to the need for a teacher of God's Word? I put one sentence that seems particularly important in bold type:

From Acts 8:26-35: *But an angel of the Lord spoke to Philip saying, "Arise and go south to the road that descends from Jerusalem to Gaza." (This is a desert road) And he arose and went; and behold, there was an Ethiopian eunuch, a court official of Candace, queen of the Ethiopians, who was in charge of all her treasure; and he had come to Jerusalem to worship. And he was returning and sitting in his chariot, and was reading the prophet Isaiah. And the Spirit said to Philip, "Go up and join this chariot." And when Philip had run up, he heard him reading Isaiah the prophet, and said, "Do you understand what you are reading?" And he said, "Well, how could I, unless someone guides me?" And he invited Philip to come up and sit with him. Now the passage of Scripture which he was reading was this: "He was led as a sheep to slaughter; and as a lamb before its shearer is silent, so He does not open His mouth. "In humiliation His judgment was taken away; who shall relate His generation? For His life is removed from the earth." And the eunuch answered Philip and said, "Please tell me of whom does the prophet say this? Of himself, or of someone else?" And Philip opened his mouth, and beginning from this Scripture he preached Jesus to him.*

The *why?* of the *encounter* is perhaps what we understand most easily. It is vital that we help young men and women see Jesus in the pages of Scripture. With so much at stake, sometimes—like Larry Walters—we can't just sit there! (By the way, "just sitting there" is one of the techniques I hope you are reminded to avoid as you help youth encounter the Bible!)

A VERY BRIEF REVIEW OF PEC

Allow me a little space for review here. The *prepare* of the Bible study experience is what the leader brings to the lesson. *Encounter* is the study that takes place during the session. The *continue* of the experience is the application of the truth learned through the Bible study after the session and almost always includes the relationship between the leader and the learner. That is why the *why?* of transformational teaching involves what many youth ministry writers call "incarnational ministry." Adults enter the world of teenagers by building relationships with them in order to minister God's love (and truth) to them. The process of transformational teaching is that adults rub shoulders with students; not becoming youth, but being in the lives of youth, just as Jesus was in our world. There are a few other *why?* questions that need to be asked. First, the *why?* of small groups. Then, *why?* we use youth to assist in the teaching process. Then, *why?* teachers vary their methods so that the effectiveness of the experience is enhanced. Finally, the *why?* of the wonder of what can happen when a caring teacher brings Scripture alive to teenagers.

JESUS' VARIETY OF TEACHING-LEARNING APPROACHES

To begin, let's look again at the Master Teacher at work in Luke 9—10. As you studied Jesus' ministry in Luke 9—10, you may have noted several examples of Jesus' multiple approaches to teaching people. His tone of voice was different for each group. For the 5000, He was compassionate and pastoral, knowing they had a myriad of needs and backgrounds. For the 70, He was urgent, almost as if He were

Our role as adults is to prepare the environment of encounter in such a way that the Word is able to intersect the lives of teenagers.

saying, "Try it and see." For the twelve, He was patient, yet a tone of accountability is present. With the three on the Mount of Transfiguration, He was desperate that they understand the unfolding plan of His Heavenly Father.

You may not have used the term "multiple approaches," but I'll bet that as you read you thought, *You know, Jesus seemed to have a knack for saying and doing just the right thing to help folks understand what He was trying to teach them.*

Why did Jesus use so many different approaches for teaching people? Why didn't He rent a lecture hall and post times for a lecture series? Why not hold a crusade in a stadium? Maybe even lead a quiet Bible study in a living room in a neighborhood? Simply stated, Jesus taught in a variety of ways because His Heavenly Father created people who learn in a variety of ways!

For example:

Physical.—In Luke 9:1-11, Jesus sent out His twelve disciples to walk through villages and to preach and heal. When they returned, they reported what they learned. Then in Luke 10:1-17, He sent out a larger crowd of disciples who "returned with joy" because they had physically done what Jesus directed them to do. Other words for physical learning are *tactile* or *experiential*. The acts of physical involvement that Jesus used are scattered throughout these two chapters: shaking the dust off of their feet in towns where they were unwelcome, the healing of the boy with the evil spirit, the disciples' act of serving the loaves and fishes, and so on. For a fun devotional exercise, go through and count the times and ways that the disciples learned by experiencing a lesson.

Logical.—Luke 9:12-17 records the reasonable conclusion the disciples drew about feeding 5000-plus people: it couldn't be done! Jesus used the same logic, however, to challenge the limits of their logic and what faith in Him could do. Even after the miracle, the disciples counted 12 baskets of leftovers! The cause and effect formula of this situation is powerful for logical/mathematical people, especially in light of the way Jesus changed their view of problem solving through His power to create and change. This is a reminder that logical thinkers may experience difficulty when the answer to a problem in a situation moves beyond a logical, problem-solving approach.

Reflective.—After Jesus prayed alone in Luke 9:18, He led His disciples to reflect on Who He was. In Luke 9:22 we see a turning point in Jesus' ministry as He began to focus on the cross and set His ministry on course for the final days in Jerusalem (v. 51). Indeed, Jesus called upon His disciples to reflect on the cost of discipleship (Luke 9:23). We can clearly see that Jesus used the example of His own life to demonstrate the characteristics of a reflective person. For example, the fact that Jesus prayed alone models reflective thinking. In His actions, we can see Jesus demonstrating a sense of being comfortable with Himself. He valued time to be alone, apart from His disciples, to focus on personal communion with His Father. The course that Jesus charted for the final part of His earthly ministry also models the goal-setting and organizational giftedness of a reflective person.

Natural.—In Luke 9:28-36, Peter, James, and John experienced the supernatural transfiguration of Jesus in a memorable natural setting—the mountain with its lightning and cloud. Such an encounter on God's mountain left an enduring impression on Peter, for he mentioned this "sacred mountain" in his last letter in 2 Peter 1:18. Something else to consider is the natural learner's capacity for classification and order. In addition to understanding and learning through natural phenomena, Gardner points out that naturalistically intelligent people have a unique ability to categorize living beings and things around them according to their common or distinctive attributes. For example, when Jesus used the illustration of the sheep and the goats in Matthew 26, He presented a vivid image for natural learners. Natural learners understand the differences in temperament and physiology that make the distinction between the animals and are able to systematize these differences to pull deep meaning from the passage. It seems important to help teachers key on this aspect of naturalistic intelligence since many nature activities could prove to be too great a challenge for Sunday-by-Sunday instruction. Also, my research indicated that, as a group, youth ministers may be lacking in this particular intelligence. Where many youth workers have no problem identifying with verbal or visual methods, it might be wise to lengthen the discussion of intelligences such as natural, physical, and reflective.

Visual.—When the disciples argued about being the greatest, Jesus dramatically moved a little child to His side. With their eyes fixed on the child, Jesus then addressed them about true greatness (Luke 9:46-48). The visual aspect of Jesus' teaching can be seen throughout this passage. The feeding of the crowd and the transfiguration were both stunning images. Imagine the impact of seeing Jesus take five little loaves of bread and two fishes and multiply them into enough food to feed the crowd and have twelve baskets of leftovers. As if that were not enough, a few days later Jesus took Peter, James, and John up a mountain and allowed them to see a glimpse of His glory. Without a doubt, Jesus understood the visual impact of these incidents, and He used them to teach the people around Him powerful truths about Himself and His power.

Relational.—Jesus sent out the 72 disciples "two by two" (Luke 10:1-4). The two-person teams could not only learn from each other but be accountable for each other, for Jesus warned that they were going out like "lambs among wolves," an illustration from nature. The gospel accounts of Jesus' ministry on earth relate many, many stories of His encounters with other people. Jesus was constantly with people and living the example of a holy life among them. Jesus taught in the context of community. He used day-to-day events and His relationship with his followers to communicate truth.

Verbal.—While Jesus used words in every teaching situation we have examined so far, in Luke 10:25-37 He answered the lawyer through telling the story of the Good Samaritan. Jesus, the Master storyteller, set the example of how to use the classic teaching method found from ancient cultures to this day—the enduring power of story.

Musical.—Finally, while the elements of music and rhythm are not evident in Luke 9–10, when the 72 returned from their assignments, Jesus broke into spontaneous praise, "full of joy and the Holy Spirit" (Luke 10:21). Matthew 26:20 clearly states that Jesus and His disciples participated in music as they sang a hymn of praise upon completing the Last Supper.

LEARNING READINESS

Jesus also understood that His hearers were at different points in their journey. When the seventy evangelists returned from their mission trip with amazing reports, they were ready for a more advanced lesson. When Peter flunked "Walking on the Water 101," his failure prepared him for a success at a later time. When we contemplate the *why?* of *encounter*, we cannot help but be amazed at how Jesus understood that some learners were ready for tougher spiritual concepts while others were still trying to grasp elementary concepts.

Many reports have been written lately about the teen brain. A predictable pattern in adolescent development is the fact that the adolescent brain has the ability to move from thinking concretely to the ability to think abstractly. For instance, in my daughter's 8-year-old thinking, the visualization of the monsters under the bed makes them very real. A late adolescent, however, may still fear the monsters under the bed, but the ability to think about the hypothetical, the potential, and the possible give the monsters a different persona.

Jesus taught in the context of community.

Psychologist Jean Piaget has identified cognitive development in teenagers in terms of:

- how a person learns to think;
- cognition being "the act of knowing or perceiving;"
- the fact that children in different age groups have different thinking patterns;
- basic movement from concrete to abstract thinking.

Piaget indicated that intelligence matures through the growth of cognitive structures that depend upon the ability to classify experiences and information. Since younger teenagers think primarily in concrete terms, the teaching methods may need to be more experiential. As teenagers get older, they begin to think in terms of pop psychology, endlessly wondering what their future holds. They tend to be idealistic, sometimes to the point of a messianic complex ("I must fix the world"). Their arena of thinking is largely egocentric, though gradually giving way to thoughts of others.

Nobody expects a Youth Sunday School teacher to be a psychologist. Most of the things in the paragraphs above are reminders of what you already know. These examples mean that we, like Jesus, must pay attention to the individual characteristics of our learners, and adjust our teaching methods accordingly.

THE WHY? GIVES WAY TO WHO?

In the next chapter, you will read that the *who?* of the encounter is unpredictable. Some weeks, we may have only our own church group teenagers. Some weeks, we may have "spend the night" guests from varied backgrounds. Some weeks, we may have only one teenager in our class. The *why?* of *encounter* demands that we resist the urge to put the prepared lesson away until more kids come. Perhaps God has led you to prepare an encounter for that one student.

I see the role of the prepared teacher in Bible study as that of a point guard in basketball. He knows the offense; he knows the plays that are available to him. The team has practiced, trying to anticipate situations that require adjustments. As he brings the ball down the floor, he doesn't get discouraged because the defense is not set up the way it is supposed to be for the play he had in mind. He adjusts, calling another play, aware of the possibilities of all of the players involved. He looks for openings—opportune moments that will allow him to take advantage of whatever the defense gives him, with the goal of scoring a basket. There are many different ways that the goal can be achieved, and many players that can be involved, but the goal is clear.

Endnotes

[1] As reported in the Los Angeles Times, Wednesday, November 24, 1993. Sadly, the reason that the story was revisited after more than eleven years was that Larry Walters had taken his own life. Shortly after his stunt, he appeared on "The Tonight Show" and was flown to New York to be on "Late Night with David Letterman," which he later described as "the most fun I've ever had." He traveled and spoke of his experience for a few years, but later slipped into despair and committed suicide.

CHAPTER 6

WHO Do We Encounter
IN A BIBLE STUDY GROUP?

When I was in Winnfield, Louisiana, serving as a minister of youth, my wife was a reporter. Judi was the news and sports editor for the *Winn Parish Enterprise*, our weekly newspaper. One of Judi's assignments was to cover the Louisiana Forest Festival. If you have ever lived in a small town, you will know that an annual community festival is a big deal. By now you are thinking, *Allen, thanks for the little trip down memory lane, but what does the Forest Festival have to do with the* who? *of encountering the word of God in a youth Bible study?*

Think about the reporter who is covering a special event like a festival. In order for that person to write an accurate story, he or she must ask some basic questions about who will attend the event. At the Forest Festival, there were woodcarvers, entrants in the logging competition, the crafts folk, the jelly-and-preserve makers, and rodeo contestants. Also attending were people who just wanted to be with their family and friends. I imagine there were also some people who simply like to attend any type of festival, regardless of the theme. Finally, there were some people who were driving by on the highway, heard all the noise, and stopped to see what was going on!

On the opposite end of the spectrum, the people who would not attend the festival would be those who had heard about it but had no interest in attending; people who had been once or twice and decided not to go back; people who intended to come, but something else came up; even people who wanted to come, but were mad at somebody so they stayed away on purpose.

A feature story would be possible about any of the people or groups of people who might attend, but to write the story, a reporter has to understand the personalities, the motivations, the background and the experiences of the characters who are the subjects of the article.

In the last chapter, we examined the *why?* of encountering God's word in a youth Bible study. *Why* would a person engage in an encounter with the Bible? *Why* do we encounter the Bible in small groups? *Why* would God allow wonderful things to happen when caring adults get knee-to-knee with needy students in small groups? In that chapter, we stopped short of dealing with the *who?* of encountering the Bible. We didn't ask the question (Stay with me here!) "Why would the *who?* come to Youth Sunday School?" Like my wife, the reporter who covered the Forest Festival, we should look around at the types of people who typically come to Bible study and consider their personalities, their families, and their interests. Inevitably, the interview of a festival attender or a Bible study attender would end with a question something along the lines of, "Why do you choose to come here when there are many other things you could be doing with your time?"

FROM FOREST FESTIVAL TO SUNDAY SCHOOL

As we look around our Sunday School class, we would benefit from a little investigative reporting. *Who?* are these kids who come here when they could be other places? Knowing that many students who are on our rolls have made the decision to stop coming, we should ask *who?* those kids are and find out what caused them to disconnect. We looked at the youth culture in chapter 2 and, hopefully, you got some help there. Now we look at the individual possibilities within your class.

Let me again affirm you as an adult who volunteers your time to work with teenagers. You, too, could be doing a lot of other things. In chapter 1, we looked at the *why?* of teaching youth in Bible study, and you have responded to that call. One of the greatest things about volunteers who work with youth is that we are as different from one another as the teenagers are from their friends. In my classes at the seminary, I preach the fact that there is tremendous advantage in having as many adults as possible involved with teenagers in our churches. If the youth minister is a "lone ranger," (doing most of the teaching and leading in the youth ministry) a risk is taken. That risk is that all students will mesh with the youth minister. If some of them do not like the youth minister or have difficulty connecting with his or her personality, those youth potentially become the students who stop attending.

If there are several diverse adults working with the teenagers, perhaps a better personality match will emerge and some of those youth will stay connected. So thanks for being you and thanks for being different. Your different approach may mesh with a student with a particular learning style. Remember that Jesus seemed to have an incredible intuition about how to teach in order to maximize the learning of an individual.

JESUS HEARS A WHO?

In the Dr. Seuss book, *Horton Hears A Who*, an elephant named Horton hears voices from a speck of dust on a clover. He vows to protect them, asserting, "I'll just have to save him. Because, after all, a person's a person, no matter how small."[1] In Luke 9-10, the passage we considered earlier, Jesus heard (and understood) the *who?* that he encountered. He understood that the crowd on the hillside was driven by its physical hunger. He understood the growing (yet still volatile) faith of the twelve. He understood the eager anticipation of the seventy. He even understood the personality of Peter who talked out loud when he should have been drinking in the awesomeness of God.

UNDERSTANDING THE UNIQUENESS OF EACH WHO? LEADS TO SPIRITUAL GROWTH

A common theme in the Scripture is that Jesus took the time to learn about people and their needs. When He was around carpenters, He talked about wood; when He was around fishermen, He talked about fish; when He was around government officials, He talked about taxes and authority. Look again at Luke 9-10 and we see that Jesus also encountered a broken-hearted father, a rich young ruler, a would-be disciple, a child as an object lesson, and his friends Martha and Mary. Even as He was interrupted, He took time to hear about the *who?* He understood what we are trying to understand about effective Bible study: that understanding the *who?* of encountering the Word unlocks comprehension in the learner.

Even among His own disciples, Jesus showed that He knew of their individual learning patterns. If youth workers will adjust and guide the *encounter* toward the learning styles of each individual in their class, the chances are greater that they will help youth *continue* in the following levels of spiritual development:

- Level 1—Cognitive (*knowledge and understanding*); Knowledge of the truth is grasped, remembered, and processed.
- Level 2—Affective (*attitudes and convictions*); Convictions, feelings, attitudes, or emotions are developed regarding the truth encountered. More about the power of emotions will be introduced in chapter 10.
- Level 3—Behavioral (*lifestyle and skills*); Changes are consciously made in behavior based upon the processing of the truth.

APPROACHES, INTELLIGENCES, AND METHODS

Before we start looking at specific approaches and methods, let's define what is meant by *approach*. An approach is the way a learner prefers to gather and process information. Some use the term *learning style* to designate such learning preferences. Learning styles include the human ability to understand truth, both

An approach is the way a learner prefers to gather and process information.

concrete and abstract. This ability grows out of the individual's physical, emotional, social, mental, and spiritual development (chapter 2). In addition, some people are concrete learners and some are conceptual learners. Remember that younger youth are moving intellectually from concrete thinking to abstract (conceptual) thinking. The wise teacher considers the younger youth's intellectual development when selecting a teaching method.

The variety of ways people prefer to learn have been categorized into learning style theories. The emphasis on learning styles grew out of secular psychology and learning theory that focused on the learner as a person.[2] For a number of years, learning styles were grouped into three broad categories: verbal, visual, and kinesthetic. Simply stated, educators observed that some people learn best verbally, others visually, and others by doing.

More recently, learning styles have been defined more sharply in terms of "intelligences." Everyone is "smart" in some way—not just verbally or logically, the traditional measurements of intelligence.[3] I like the idea that was first suggested by Howard Gardner, a professor at Harvard University. He suggested that there are eight learning-teaching approaches: *verbal, logical, visual, physical, musical, relational, reflective,* and *natural.* Gardner called these "intelligences" or certain abilities that enable us to learn, understand, and deal with new situations.[4] I think of the eight intelligences as personal information processing strategies. These intelligences are different from learning style theories because they attempt to sum up how we internalize, process, and turn out products of worth. These intelligences are common to all of us, and could be indicators of our learning styles.

As teenagers grow older and move toward adulthood, different intelligences begin to dominate the way they learn best. Gardner's eight intelligences are:

- Relational/Interpersonal—(*People Smart*)—learning by interaction with others, working in groups, presentations, demonstrations, discussions
- Musical/Rhythmic—(*Music Smart*)—learning by singing, listening to music, playing instruments
- Logical/Mathematical—(*Logic Smart*)—learning by problem solving, asking questions, experimentation, debate
- Natural/Biological—(*Nature Smart*)—learning by classifying nature, exploring and processing outdoors, metaphors with biological and natural
- Physical/Kinesthetic—(*Body Smart*)—learning by dance, exercise, drama, role play, sports
- Reflective/Intrapersonal—(*Self Smart*)—learning by meditation, thinking deeply, goal setting, guided daydreaming
- Visual/Spatial—(*Picture Smart*)—learning by painting, drawing, reading maps, making patterns, or designs
- Verbal/Linguistic—(*Word smart*)—learning by writing, speaking, reading, listening

We choose to use the term *approach* for learning style. While every person has a dominant approach to learning, everyone can learn through a combination of several approaches, even simultaneously. Beginning with the biblical principle that the Holy Spirit is the ultimate Teacher of spiritual Truth, we identify eight approaches to learning and teaching God's Word. In the following paragraphs, each approach is described with an example of a Bible person who typifies this approach.

⊛ RELATIONAL
These learners are highly social, make friends easily, and may be very good talkers. They are keen observers of others, noticing their moods and motivations. Recognizing how people feel enables relational individuals to respond

Beginning with the biblical principle that the Holy Spirit is the ultimate Teacher of spiritual truth, we identify eight approaches to learning and teaching God's Word.

accordingly. Relational (interpersonal) learners are aided in processing information meaningfully when they are able to "see things through the eyes of others." They are drawn to activities that allow them to cooperate and interact with others. They may be known as "people persons." In the Book of Acts, Joseph of Cyprus was renamed Barnabas (The Encourager) because of the way he related to the church, its ministry, and to other Christians like John Mark.

♫ MUSICAL

Many people enjoy music. Some people seem more sensitive to rhythm and pitch than others. They tend to be good listeners. Because they are more comfortable with music, singing and movement are their natural responses to music. They are aided by music that is collateral to the experience (background music in a video, mood music, etc.). It has also been observed that many musical learners have music "playing" in their minds a great deal of the time. Discerning whether a student lives life with an "internal soundtrack" can be a helpful indicator of musical learning preference. These learners may learn new songs quickly and remember them easily. They find it easy to express themselves through music—composing, playing, and performing. As David penned his psalms, he expressed his faith in a musical form. His words form the basis for many contemporary choruses and hymns of praise.

One additional thought about music—culturally, youth are at a time in life where music is of extreme importance. All youth have the ability to memorize music and music videos with mind-boggling proficiency. Studies have shown that music is particularly influential during adolescence. Such influence should not be confused with musical intelligence in the sense of a "personal learning strategy."

✿ LOGICAL

Problem solving is an enjoyable experience for some learners. They see patterns in the world and can reason through difficult situations. These learners rely heavily on analogies. They like working with abstractions and may be gifted in the field of mathematics. They enjoy games and puzzles, even jokes with odd punch lines. (For

example, "If a plane crashes on the border between Texas and Oklahoma, where should they bury the survivors?")[6]

When making a point to his readers, Paul often used a very logical argument or formal debate style. He stated evidence from the Old Testament. He appealed to logic and reason in matters of grace and faith. The Book of Romans is an example of approaching learning and teaching through logic. The use of rhetoric in the book of Job also represents such logic.

NATURAL

These learners enjoy the beauty of God's creation. They are skilled at identifying elements of the natural world. They may relate well to stories in the Bible that allude to elements in nature. Investigation and exploration of God's world are appealing to these learners. They have an interest in plants and animals and a high sensitivity for the stewardship of God's world. Many of the Psalms approach teaching and learning from a sensitivity to the natural world. Don't forget the classification ability of the natural learner. In addition to learning from nature, these learners are able to discern patterns of behavior, weather, growth, and so on. This ability can be central to the learner's ability to identify with the motives and behavior of characters in Scripture. Psalm 8, 23, and 139 are all examples of David's experience with God and His mighty works. David saw God active in nature all around him.

PHYSICAL

Persons who approach learning from a physical standpoint are very active and may have good coordination. When they tell a story, they not only tell it, they play it out. Physical learners also may be inclined to learn through mission projects or other helping activities. They like to use their physical abilities and skills in sports and drama. Fine motor skills are also a part of this intelligence, and projects that involve the hands are very appropriate for this type of learner. Ezekiel has been described as an ecstatic kind of prophet. His unique approach to "forth telling" and "foretelling" drew great attention during his ministry. He acted out many of his prophecies to make points that were memorable in the minds and lives of his contemporaries. I also think Thomas was a physical (tactile) learner because Jesus instructed him to put his fingers in the nail prints in the Savior's hands and to place his hands in the pierced side.

REFLECTIVE

Reflective learners tend to understand who they are and how they feel. They also have a high level of comfort with their own identity. Working alone may be their desire. People who have this approach to learning do not actively shun the company of others, but often choose activities that allow self-expression. These people also are comfortable with extended periods of solitude. They may internalize concepts by personalizing them. They also may be self-starters who are very comfortable in setting goals and working with purpose to achieve those goals. During the significant times in the life of Mary, the Gospels portray her as a woman who pondered God's will and her role in His plan. She found times of reflection to be her own personal teachable moments. Who could forget these famous words of reflection?

And Mary said: "My soul exalts the Lord, And my spirit has rejoiced in God my Savior. For He has had regard for the humble state of His bondslave; for behold, from this time on all generations will count me blessed. For the Mighty One has done great things for me; and holy is His name. And His mercy is upon generation after generation toward those who fear Him. He has done mighty deeds with His arm; He has scattered those who were proud in the thoughts of their heart. He has brought down rulers from their thrones, and has exalted those who were humble. He has filled the hungry with good things; and sent away the rich empty-handed. He has given help to Israel His servant, in remembrance of His mercy, As He spoke to our fathers, to Abraham and his offspring forever." (Luke 1:46-55)

👓 VISUAL

Visual learners can "see" in their imaginations as well as in the concrete world. Their visual understanding includes space and distance concepts. They also enjoy creating their own pictures and visual representations of what they are learning. This learning approach also involves the anticipation of mental images. This part of spatial intelligence explains why some athletes are able to "see the entire playing field" and to anticipate the movements and actions of other players. Visual arts, videos, television, and film foster productive means of learning for these individuals. As he wrote the Gospels, epistles, and Revelation, John used vivid images to paint pictures for his readers. Light and darkness were just two of the elements John used to teach his followers about God and godliness.

☎ VERBAL

Even though a constant diet of lecture is not the most effective teaching methodology, some of your class members will be verbal learners. *Verbal* in this sense is both spoken and written. These learners listen, and they read, as the teacher provides details during the lesson. They learn through the use of stories, panel discussions, debates, interviews, brainstorming, and open-ended questions. They also demonstrate a heightened ability to persuade and negotiate with others. Verbal learners are comfortable with reading aloud, composing poetry, and presenting verbal descriptions of biblical events. Verbal learners like the sounds of words and may have large vocabularies. Solomon's writings serve as an example of an individual who approached learning from a verbal perspective. His speech at the dedication of the Temple in 1 Kings 8 demonstrates a verbal approach to learning and teaching. Paul was a verbal learner—his vivid descriptions of events in the book of Acts reveal him as a person fluent in the use of words.

TEACHING METHODS AND LEARNING APPROACHES

Examine the "Approaches to learning and teaching" chart in the appendix. Note how under each column there is a way youth learn. For example, under "Relational" you will find in the first box that "Learners Clarify." Then you will see an example of a method teachers can use to address this learning approach. Note the wide variety of both learning approaches that youth have and teaching methods that you could employ. Keep in mind, too, that this chart is representative, not exhaustive, of possible approaches to how youth learn and how to teach them. There is virtually no limit to how the Holy Spirit may work to impress God's Truth upon a teenager's heart and life! See the appendix for a list of possible teaching methods grouped by different categories.

WHEW! NOW THINK ABOUT YOUR OWN KIDS!

Now think about youth you are around or those whom you teach. Try to write a teenager's name beside each of the eight teaching-learning approaches. (By the way, did you identify your own learning approach?) Remember—no individual

There is virtually no limit to how the Holy Spirit may work to impress God's Truth upon a teenager's heart and life!

learns through only one of these approaches. Think of the combination of dominant and secondary intelligence patterns as a kind of intelligence profile. This means that each person will have varying degrees of strength and weakness for all of the eight intelligences. Two or three will generally be primary for the individual, with each person possessing moderate to low degrees of the other intelligences.

Youth will gain some level of benefit from instruction that corresponds to intelligences in which they are moderately gifted. Instruction may also further enhance the dominant intelligence or ability. Learning approach preferences may change as the person grows older or develops new skills and interests.

Youth learn in a variety of ways. One approach won't fit all youth! Wise teachers will plan to use a variety of teaching approaches to involve the most youth in ways they like to learn best. As teachers grow in their relationships with learners, they begin to identify preferred approaches to learning. By using a variety of approaches, teachers can determine which approach is most effective with learners in their class. When teachers teach in ways God has gifted learners, learning is most effective and learners are inclined to participate in the teaching-learning process for spiritual transformation. The Holy Spirit will play an important role in the life of the teacher in guiding the teacher toward a better understanding of the learners and their individual approaches.

GROUND RULES, DISCIPLINE, AND THINGS YOU DIDN'T PLAN ON

Establishing ground rules for a Bible study group is one way to keep relationships strong and focused on biblical instruction. Lynn Pryor, a LifeWay Youth Sunday School employee and director of a seventh-grade Sunday School department, prominently posts these ground rules for his younger youth. (They may be easily adapted for older youth.)

1. No slams.
2. There's no such thing as a stupid question.
3. No one talks when someone else is talking. (That is, only one person speaks at a time.)

Being proactive to develop a teaching plan that addresses the variety of ways youth prefer to learn can help head off most discipline problems. Also, communicating your knowledge, passion, and joy in Bible study will help youth stay focused as they see your enthusiasm for God's Word. Nevertheless, discipline problems come up in every teacher's experience. Even Jesus had discipline problems when He taught. Do you recall Luke 9:46 and the argument that broke out among His disciples about who would be the greatest? Jesus redirected their attention through the object lesson of a little child.

What are some principles for handling discipline problems during a session? Yount offers suggestions that are sound for any classroom situation.[7]

1. Use positive language. For example, say, "Speak one at a time," instead of "Don't everybody talk at once."

2. Change the pace. (That usually means to speed up.) Move on to the next teaching activity.

3. Control objects that distract students' attention.

4. Redirect students' attention to the subject through such actions as asking a question or giving verbal hints. Making demands and stating logical consequences should be your last resort. If you do have to exercise the logical consequences of breaking a guideline, be sure the consequence fits the crime and be sure it is consistently enforced. Avoid banning a teen from a Bible study group.

5. Give students opportunity for self-control. It often helps to physically move next to the misbehaving party. An appropriate, non-aggressive touch, such as a hand on the shoulder, could help redirect the student, especially a younger youth. Never, however, use touch with a visibly angry student or a member of the opposite sex. Due to the potential for litigation (yes, even against churches), if you consistently have discipline problems, make sure there is another adult sitting in your session both to help you with his or her presence and to offer support in case a student makes an accusation of abuse. Some churches are also constructing doors with windows so that people can observe a small group during a session.

6. You must control yourself. James 1:19 speaks of being "slow to become angry for man's anger does not bring about the righteous life that God desires." In all areas of teaching, but especially discipline, the leader is the lesson.

For an inexperienced leader, the prospect of having to discipline a student can be frightening. For the most experienced teacher, handling discipline situations is frustrating and distracting. There are no easy answers, but here are a few reminders:[8]

1. Work on relationships first. When you have a genuine relationship with a teenager, you are more likely to receive a positive response if and when you have to get tough with them. If youth know that you care about them and have their best interests in mind, they are more likely to follow your leadership.

2. Seek to understand individual youth. Sometimes we expect the kids in our class this year to be like the kids from last year, or we may compare one youth with another in the class. With the volatile nature of the adolescent years, it may not even be reasonable to compare a student today with how he or she was yesterday!

3. Let youth be youth. Normal youth are noisy, active, and easily distracted. Expecting youth to behave like adults is expecting the impossible. *Controlled chaos* may be a more accurate description of youth's learning experiences than a quiet, orderly situation that exists only in your dreams.

4. Make the guidelines clear. It is vital that we set and maintain clear expectations

In all areas of teaching, but especially discipline, the leader is the lesson.

of youth and their behavior. Who sets these guidelines? You and your youth should collaborate, and negotiate, but never retaliate. Youth tend to support what they help create. Work together with them to decide what should be expected of them during worship, study sessions, retreats, or fellowships. One of the best things we can do for youth is to help them understand the process of setting limits.

5. Be sure the consequence fits the crime. If you are going to set guidelines for behavior, spell out the consequences for violating the guidelines. Decide the *non*negotiables—like possession of illegal drugs, alcohol, or weapons. Spell out beforehand what the "send out or send home" offenses are, so if and when you have to remove a student from a class or event, the discipline doesn't seem arbitrary.

TOUGH LOVE AND TRANSFORMATION

Spiritual transformation is God's work, and as a youth leader you will want to "speak the truth in love," even tough love. Remember that relationships with youth are important. Privately, devote some individual attention to the misbehaving youth outside the Bible study session. Seek to understand the youth and his family. Speak with parents and involve parents in meeting with the youth as you need to. Finally, consider involving other youth as mentors to the youth during or after the session, especially if you have a group made up of all ages of youth. Younger youth often have high regard for older youth who devote time to them.

There are also times when a youth shares with you something personal or emotional that you did not expect. Examples include a student whose family is going to move, a parent's affair, a sister's unwanted pregnancy, a serious illness, a death of a loved one (including a pet), or divorce. A student may express grief over fractured friendships, especially boy-girl crises. Much wisdom is needed to discern how much time to devote to dealing with the personal crisis during the session. Certainly, you want to take every expression seriously and you should communicate genuine concern for the welfare of the teenager and his or her family. Arrange a later time to talk on the phone or meet in a public place. Avoid meeting alone with members of the opposite sex. Keep the student focused on Scripture promises and biblical resources for dealing with youth life issues. One of the best resources is *The 24-Hour Counselor* CD-ROM that addresses 24 of the top problems teenagers face. On this CD-ROM there also is a video including the plan of salvation.[9]

Sometimes youth ask a question you can't answer. Rather than faking it (which youth can always see through), thank them for the question, admit to them that you don't know the answer, and promise to do some research to try to answer the question. Consider giving them an assignment, such as to use a Bible concordance or Bible dictionary, and call or email the student before the next session. Then consider giving a report to the group at the next session.

Sometimes a student will complain about the curriculum. When a student says, "I've studied this story all my life!" consider responding by asking them kindly to tell the story themselves. Point out to them that they have never studied the story as a seventh-grader or tenth-grader, for example. Add that God's Word is active and alive (Heb. 4:12) and speaks to us at every stage of life.

WHO IS IN A SUNDAY SCHOOL BIBLE STUDY GROUP?

At the heart of the teaching strategy for Sunday School is the creation of "open" Bible study groups for teaching both believers and unbelievers. In general, to be

open means to be *characterized by ready accessibility for a particular purpose; not shut or locked; having no enclosing or confining barrier.* In the context of the grouping and grading plan for a local church's Bible teaching ministry, "open" means both believers and unbelievers are invited to participate in a Bible study class, department, study group, small group, cell group, or event that has an intentional evangelistic purpose—every time the group meets.

An open Bible study group also assimilates people into the local church. At the same time, an open group intentionally focuses on sending out members as witnesses and leaders of new groups. In other words, open groups are open on both ends. They are conduits of the gospel enterprise—receiving, assimilating, providing a base for discipling, and then sending out. Finally, an open group should be defined by its purpose, nature, and function. Here's how the concept of an open Bible study group applies to Youth Sunday School. Youth Sunday School groups *are*:

- "Open" groups, meaning that both believers and unbelievers are invited to participate every time the group meets. Youth Sunday School groups can symbolize this openness by always leaving a vacant chair in the group and asking, "Who should be in this chair the next time we meet?"
- Groups that study God's Word with an intentional focus on leading youth to faith in Christ, helping them feel a part of the church, and encouraging them to lead others to Christ.
- Groups that do not expect or require advanced preparation by participants. Students can come anytime whether they know anything about church, God, or the Bible. Bible study leaders will introduce youth to biblical truth that can transform their lives during and after the session.
- Groups that call leaders to *prepare* themselves before the session and lead the participants to *encounter* God's Word during the session and then *continue* to learn and obey God's Word in daily living and family relationships after the session. One way to continue learning and obedience is by directing participants to go deeper into evangelism, discipleship, fellowship, ministry, worship, and missions through other opportunities in the church and youth ministry, such as discipleship, music, and missions groups.
- Groups that produce adult and youth leaders who start new small groups.

• Groups that, for purposes of accountability for evangelism, discipleship, fellowship, ministry, and discipleship beyond the session, are composed of one or two adult leaders with the same gender students. From time to time for the sake of variety, students can be grouped in a variety of ways, including coed, during the study session.

Youth Sunday School groups are *not*:

• Focused only on the needs of members.

• Focused on content that is not Bible study. There is a legitimate need for such groups to focus on specific Bible study and discipleship content, crisis support, or skill development, but Youth Sunday School groups focus their ministry on people reaching and ministering to people who are both inside and outside the group.

And finally . . . . .

Now that you've heard all the *who?* of *encounter* that you can stand for now; as we move into the *what?* and *how?* of *encounter*, prepare to move more into the methodology of the *encounter* event.

_____

Endnotes

[1] (Dr.) Theodore Seuss, *Horton Hears A Who*©1954. New York: Random House, Inc., 6.

[2] William R. Yount, *Called to Teach*. Nashville: Broadman and Holman, 1999,176.

[3] Thomas Armstrong, *7 Kinds of Smart, Identifying and Developing Your Multiple Intelligences, Revised and Updated with Information on 2 New Kinds of Smart*. New York: Penguin Books, 1999, 9.

[4] Dr. Rick Morton, who did his doctoral research on Gardner's Multiple Intelligences (MI) reminded me that Gardner asserts MI begins and ends in a different place than other learning style theories. Most learning style theories assume that abilities like discernment and memory are similar across all types of content and MI assumes that abilities are intelligence related. For example, a music smart person will likely remember and value music-related instruction better than instruction related to an intelligence in which they are weaker.

[5] Gardner did not really intend that MI would be applied as a learning style theory. Armstrong (see above note) and David Lazear, in further research, made this connection.

[6] If you, like me, are totally devoid of problem-solving skills, I will tell you the punchline. I don't want to hang you up from reading the rest of the book—*They don't have to bury the survivors!*

[7] Yount, 158-165.

[8] *Connected, Committed, and A Little Bit Crazy: Teaching Youth the Bible*, Allen Jackson and Randy Johnson. Nashville: Convention Press, 1996,107.

[9] Available through LifeWay Christian Stores, 1-800-458-2772, or online at www.lifeway.com/order/index.asp.

CHAPTER 7

WHAT HAPPENS WHEN WE ENCOUNTER
GOD'S WORD IN A YOUTH BIBLE STUDY GROUP?

Have you ever asked youth why they come to Sunday School? In an informal survey conducted in October 1999 with 13 churches from Virginia to Hawaii, youth were asked to rank the top reasons they attended Sunday School. (The survey form is found on the "Youth Information Sheet" page in the appendix.) One-third of the students selected "to study and learn the Bible" as the top reason.

At the same time, one-fourth of the youth chose "to be with their friends at church or a friend invited me" as the second reason. The peer group can play an important and positive role in a teenager's decision to come to a Bible study group. Once involved in an open Bible study group, the youth can move toward experiencing biblical fellowship (*koinonia*)—one of the five functions of the church.

Also important in this survey is what youth said about the family. Not far behind being with friends (25.6%) was "as a family, we always come and being a part of my family is important to me" (22.6%). Addressing the strategic principle of family responsibility outside the session is an important factor in youth coming to Bible study.

Finally, the survey reveals that one out of ten youth said that caring adults impact their decision to come to Sunday School. The responsiveness to caring adults seemed to increase as youth moved from middle school to high school. As an adult, you can make a difference!

To lead youth to faith in Christ and build them as Great Commission Christians, we must provide a quality Bible study experience during the session. We must also focus on relationships with and among youth before, during, and after the session. Finally, ministry with parents and family members is critical to the ongoing success of a Youth Sunday School ministry. As important as relationships are,

Teaching
and learning
can occur
before
the session,
during
the session,
and after
the session.

however, poorly led Bible study sessions can empty more classrooms than good relationships can fill.

This chapter examines what keeps youth engaged in a quality Bible study session. What goes on during a 60-minute session in which an adult leader guides youth toward spiritual transformation through an encounter with God's Word in a Bible study group?

TIME IS OF THE ESSENCE

Time is an important factor in teaching youth God's Word. Typically, a team of Youth Sunday School leaders will have only a 60-minute session. Contrast this brief amount of time with the multiplied hours of media youth experience during the week—computers, TV, and music—and Sunday School leaders must make every minute count![1]

At this point, thinking in terms of units of study, not just sessions, is helpful. Units can range from one to six sessions. While each session can stand alone, teaching youth with the unit in mind will help you avoid needless repetition from session to session. Teaching with a view to the unit will also help you plan *continue* activities that may take more than one week to implement. There will be more on *continue* in chapters 11 and 12, but for now, remember that Sunday School is not a once-a-week event but a seven-day-a-week strategy. Your LifeWay Youth Sunday School leader guides have unit pages to help you think beyond just one session.

To maximize the time allotted for a Youth Sunday School session, however, Sunday School for a New Century resources employ a concept for Bible study groups that has proven effective for the last 30 years—total period teaching. In total period teaching, teaching and learning begins when the first student arrives. All of the time set aside for Sunday School—the total period—is teaching time. That's why you want to think, *as youth arrive*, and *when youth leave*, when you plan and lead your session. Even the announcements can be creatively related to the "Biblical Truth" for that session.

At the same time, because Sunday School by definition is a *strategy*, not a session, teaching is not limited to 60 minutes every time the group meets. Teaching and learning can occur before the session, during the session, and after the session. In short, teaching youth the Bible is a total period teaching strategy. The best "teachable moments" may be after the session on the phone, in personal conversation, through the mail, by email, or on the Internet. Think "seven days" not "sixty minutes"!

Nevertheless, what happens during the Bible study session is critical. This chapter and the next will focus on what happens during the 60-minute session. Chapters 11 and 12 will deal with what happens after the session.

KEY TERMS IN OPEN BIBLE STUDY GROUP RESOURCES

Beginning with the Fall 2000 LifeWay Youth Sunday School resources, you will find terms that help you keep your Bible study group open and focused on God's Word. All of these terms will be in all Youth Sunday School leader guides, and some will be in the learner guides.

- *Session Date.*—Family Bible Study curriculum materials are designed for use in a particular quarter. Consequently, you will find the term, "week of . . ." to identify the date for the session. Yet, because Youth Sunday School is not simply a once-a-week event, the words, "week of . . ." will remind you and youth that the Bible study begins with an *encounter* during the session and *continues* after the session. Also, you could choose to conduct the actual session on any day during that week you gather students, not just Sunday.

  LifeTrak resources have no dates prescribed. You can teach the session in the sequence they appear in the leader guide or you may change the sequence. You could even lead the sessions in other settings, such as a retreat or Wednesday night, or in any quarter you choose. Regardless, all LifeTrak sessions employ the same strategy of *encountering* and *continuing* to guide students to live God's Word in their daily relationships.

- *Session Title.*—An attention-getting title seeks to pique student interest in the study. The title may create conflict or introduce the content of the session.
- *Life Question.*—The "Life Question" will help youth grasp the significance and relevance of the "Bible Passage" and "Biblical Truth" for their lives. The "Life Question" will encourage youth to discern what God's message is for them through this study. At some point during the session (usually near the beginning) the Bible study session should help youth acknowledge the authority that rules what they think, believe, feel, and the way they behave. The "Life Question" will position them to hear God's answer to the question, *What is God's message for me through this study?*
- *Bible Passage.*—The Scripture reference of the passage to be studied is listed.
- *Key Verse.*—The "Key Verse" reflects the "Biblical Truth" and/or answers the "Life Question." In Youth Sunday School, this verse is also the recommended memory verse for the session.
- *Biblical Setting.*—This brief statement of the Bible passage's setting, context, and/or background will help leaders and learners understand its relationship to the larger message of the Bible.
- *Biblical Truth.*—This is a statement of the abiding biblical truth being focused upon in the session. At times in Family Bible Study, the "Biblical Truth" will also relate the session's truth to the common Bible study plan for all ages and help youth place the Bible passage truth(s) in relationship to the larger biblical worldview.
- *Life Impact.*—These brief statements identify ways both leaders and learners will give evidence of spiritual transformation in their lives. The statements could also indicate ways participants could contribute to Christ's work through the church as a result of the study. The statements may reflect the biblical content (*Search the Truth* for what the Bible said to its first readers) and biblical concepts (*Discover the Truth* for understanding what the Bible means in terms of eternal principles) examined during the Bible study. Yet, spiritual transformation must move beyond making a mental connection of a biblical truth's relevance. Obedience in the lives of leaders and learners will occur as participants *Struggle with the Truth*, *Believe the Truth*, and *Obey the Truth* every day of the week. The "Life Impact" statements give direction for preparing to study and teach the session and suggest, without prescribing, ways in which God's Spirit uses His Word to transform lives.

WHAT HAPPENS DURING THE SESSION?

A good Bible study session is more than just a well-executed teaching plan. While good sessions begin with good preparation, what the students actually experience intellectually (what they think) and emotionally (what they feel) during the session will usually determine what they do behaviorally after the session as they *continue* to learn and live. What characterizes a good "open" youth Bible study session? Four characteristics stand out:

1. *Every student is loved as an individual and wanted.*—The role of the teacher is to guide learning in ways that facilitate the work of the Holy Spirit to transform learners' lives. Transformational teaching includes recognizing the ways in which

The "Life Question" will encourage youth to discern what God's message is for them through this study.

youth learn best. Chapters 2, 6, and 10 can serve as a handy reference for understanding youth and how they learn. Yet, to determine how your youth learn best, you must get to know them as individuals, and that begins with observing their likes, dislikes, successes, and struggles.

To begin, remember that you, as an adult, are from a different generation. As an adult, you may sometimes feel like an international missionary who doesn't dress like youth do, eat the food youth do, or even speak the language youth do! Yet, if you are willing to listen, learn, and accept generational and individual differences, you will position yourself for God to work through you to love and teach them.

Have you observed that teenagers today typically process information differently than most of us adults? If we adults fail to teach in a way that addresses their ability to gather large amounts of information in a very rapid manner, we may run the risk of boring kids with a pace that is good for us but too slow for them.

New Testament teachers related to their learners, both personally and creatively in language, culture, and life needs. Jesus was open and approachable to individuals, allowing questions and challenges to His teaching. He taught individuals, small groups, or large groups in any setting at any time. He used everyday objects and stories to grab the attention of His hearers. He loved individuals as they were, even His adversaries, but also sought to lead individuals to be what God created them to be. At Pentecost, Peter began with what people were experiencing. In Athens Paul started with what his hearers knew from secular philosophy. Taken together, Jesus, Peter, and Paul illustrate what you as a youth Bible teacher have to do today: Start where youth are and then creatively focus their attention on biblical truth.

The depth of relationship that you have with each individual learner can affect how well that learner will be motivated to participate in the Bible study session. One practical reason to keep classes small is so you and the other leaders can personally attend to individual needs. After all, Jesus chose only 12 disciples, and even within the 12, He devoted special time to three. We at LifeWay recommend that a youth Bible study small group or class be limited to 12 youth enrolled. In such a class, you'll typically have four who come all the time, four who come some of the time, and four who never come. Have you thought of the fact that God has also called you to teach the youth who are *not* there? Following Jesus' example in Luke 9, Great Commission teachers go where the kids are (v. 4), including "Samaria" (v. 52).

Classes can be grouped into larger Bible study groups called departments. Typically, departments should be no larger than five classes or 60 youth enrolled. When you reach 12 youth enrolled per class or 60 enrolled per department, start planning to create a new class or department—one of the characteristics of "open" groups discussed at the end of chapter 6. Experience has shown, by the way, that new classes usually grow faster than older ones.

How can your attention to individuals make a difference during a Bible study session? Leaders and students who learn individual names and who go out of their way to greet newcomers are demonstrating that every youth is loved and wanted. Also, teachers know the issues to address when they know the individuals. Here are some real-life examples:

- Mary learned about the death of a special grandmother to one of the girls in her Sunday School class. In addition to sending her a personal card, Mary went to the funeral. When the girl saw Mary, she said, "I didn't know when you would be here, but I knew you would come." How motivated to learn do you believe that girl will be in the next Sunday School session?

- One Sunday evening, a parent revealed to a youth teacher that his high school daughter was not planning to come to Sunday School that morning. He went on to add, however, that when she received her teacher's letter informing her that

the upcoming lesson would examine what the Scriptures teach about marriage and divorce, his daughter changed her mind and attended the session. The parent added that the session spoke to his daughter about putting a broken dating relationship behind her and helped her determine to focus anew on pursuing the college scholarship that lay within her grasp.

• Susan was shy and was sporadic in attendance. On one Sunday morning, Joe, an active youth in Sunday School, saw her sitting alone and began to engage her in lively conversation. While they went to separate classes that morning, Susan's teacher remarked how much more involved Susan was in the Bible study. Could it be that one student who took time to talk with her was the key to Susan's good Bible study experience?

2. *The session flows so that leaders and learners remain focused on God's Word.*— Do you recall the section in chapter 4, "Put Together Your Plan: Go With the Flow"? During a good Bible study session, both the leader and the learners sense that the session is going somewhere, not just drifting from one activity or topic to the next or just centered around one or two persons' need to talk. The leader's job is to guide the session so that youth engage in the biblical process of instruction as they acknowledge the authority in their lives and search, discover, personalize, struggle with, believe, and ultimately obey the Lord. Practically speaking, the leader's task is to keep the group centered on the "Biblical Truth" for the session and moving toward one or more of the proposed "Life Impact" statements in the leader's guide or one that you develop. To this end, a good session flows from getting started to getting into the Truth to getting the Truth into us. (See the "Encounter" section on the Youth Sunday School Plan Sheet in the appendix.)

• Getting Started

As youth enter the room, they should sense that the Bible study session is designed especially for them to encounter other students, adults who care, and ultimately God Himself. Be creative with room arrangements so that chairs, posters, music, and even focal walls make the room say, "We're glad you're here!" and then direct attention to the "Biblical Truth" for that session and unit.

Don't be afraid to involve all five senses, too. Preferred learning-teaching

approaches relate directly to the five senses. Youth who are musical learners will immediately notice the music that is playing when they enter. Relational learners will be concerned that "Nobody's here!" while reflective learners will not mind entering the room first and taking a seat by themselves. How the room looks, feels, sounds, and even smells will impact the teenager, especially the first-time participant. Taste is often a good way to connect with youth, too. Instead of having the traditional donuts, serve salty snacks, for example, as a way to introduce youth to a Bible study on thirsting after God. Finally, make sure you change the room arrangement from time to time to add variety.

From the earliest part of the session, the leader is the lesson. The leader's smile, enthusiasm, positive attitude, creativity, promptness to arrive before the first student, and sincere love prepare the environment for ministry and learning. The preparation of the room, including creative use of music, technology, approaches to gathering records, approaches to announcements, and, as desirable, food all are a part of getting started toward transformational teaching.

Great Commission teachers also utilize the value of organization and sharing the leadership with other adults and key youth as student leaders. All adult leaders and key student leaders should readily engage in the ministry of hospitality to make sure everyone who comes feels welcome and wanted.

Initial teaching activities, usually during a large-group Department Time, grab teenagers' attention based on where they are "coming from" in order to engage them more readily in the Bible study session. The beginning activity also should create the ministry environment by helping students and adults relate to each other so students focus their attention on learning a biblical truth that connects with their lives.

• Getting into the Truth

The next teaching activities, usually during a small-group class time, engage youth in the Bible Passage by searching the Scriptures for biblical content and biblical concepts that can be personalized for life today.

• Getting the Truth into Us

These teaching activities help youth personalize the truth of God's Word as they experience the inner conflict when biblical truth intersects with their lives today. As the Holy Spirit works in learners' lives, inner conflicts are resolved by a change of belief, attitude, and action as reflected in a lifestyle of love, trust, and obedience that glorifies God.

This flow remains similar to what we have called for years the three educational essentials of Youth Sunday School: Motivation, Examination, and Application. As noted, Sunday School is much more than a one-hour session. We can begin motivation, examination, and application in a 60-minute teaching session, but we will not complete them during the session. We may have inadvertently communicated that once youth have made a mental connection ("application") of the biblical truth to life during a session, we have done Bible study. Such a truncated approach to Bible study may be one reason why Christian youth attitudes and behaviors are not significantly different from the secular youth culture, especially in areas of lying and cheating.[2]

In addition, motivation, examination, and application do not always occur in this sequence. The Holy Spirit is ultimately the One who convicts (motivation and application) and who teaches (examination). The Holy Spirit may first lead us to examine the Scriptures that lead us to be motivated to apply them. Often applications of Scripture are made as the Scriptures are being examined. In Sunday School for a New Century materials, we are defining "application to life" in terms of the seven Bible teaching elements. "Application" moves beyond "Personalizing the Truth" (a mental connection) to "Struggling with the Truth," "Believing the Truth," and "Obeying the Truth." "Acknowledge Authority" is a key Bible teaching element because when people acknowledge what is most important in their lives and then allow the Holy Spirit to bring change of mind (repentance) and belief (conviction) that results in obedience, only then there will be genuine change from a secular worldview to the biblical worldview.

With regard to the 60-minute session itself, it generally flows from getting started to getting into the Truth of God's Word to experiencing the Truth of God's Word getting into us—both leaders and learners. The total period teaching philosophy begs for leading the session in such a way that all teaching-learning activities relate to each other—whether they are done in large-group settings (department time) or small-group settings (class time). Also, total period teaching takes a broader look to make sure each teaching-learning activity has a place in the biblical process of instruction. The goal of all teaching is to spiritually transform lives.

In summary, here are some tips for turning on the flow of a good Bible teaching session:

- From the moment youth arrive, think *as youth arrive* and choose activities for department time or class time to build relationships, direct their attention to the session's "Biblical Truth," and seek to discover what controls ("Acknowledge Authority") everyone's attitudes and beliefs about the Bible truth to be examined.
- Then guide students to understand what the Bible passage meant when it was written and its eternal truth(s) for all generations ("Search the Truth" and "Discover the Truth").
- Help students apply the passage through everyday examples of what youth should be, feel, and do as they "Personalize the Truth."
- Remember, though, that application is not complete until participants "Struggle with the Truth," "Believe the Truth," and "Obey the Truth"—which almost always comes after the session *when youth leave.*
- Avoid being so wedded to your teaching plan that you cannot address questions or issues that arise. Be ready to admit your limitations by saying, "I don't know the answer, but let's work on researching it this week."
- Finally, teach from your Bible using the personal notes you have made, and using your leader guide, learner guide, and leader pack as tools to enhance the Bible study.

3. *Youth are taught in a variety of ways.*—The death knell for any youth Bible study group is the label *boring,* and boredom is brought on by predictability. Avoid doing anything—even the most fun things—the same way every Bible study session. The worst teaching method is one that a teacher uses all the time.

Another way of saying this is not to let your teaching ministry get into a rut. A rut is a grave with both ends kicked out, and no one wants to be in a dead Sunday School class or department! One of the best ways to stay out of the rut is to vary the sequence of your groupings.

Department time is when you have all the classes together for a large-group experience. If you are in a department with multiple classes, you can vary whether you start in department time or class time. If you have one class for all youth, you could apply these principles for forming teams of two to four students within your class, perhaps by naming a student team leader. You could then move from class time to team time or team time to class time.

Advantages of department time:
- Because most youth like to be where the crowd is, there is generally a higher sense of energy and excitement, especially if you provide music and food.
- Many youth, especially first-time guests, prefer a larger group that gives them more anonymity.

The goal of all teaching is to spiritually transform lives.

Adding variety to how you group teenagers during the session will add life to your department.

• Promotion of youth department, youth ministry, or church-wide events can be delivered so that everyone hears the same thing at the same time.
• Department time is almost always coed, and enables you to get boys' and girls' perspectives.

Advantages of class time:
• Because the group is smaller, more youth can participate.
• Smaller groups tend to overcome individual differences in learning approaches and understanding. For example, youth will more likely ask a question or admit their confusion in a smaller group. Ideas, especially complex ones, can be explained more thoroughly and specifically.
• Youth, including first-time guests, want to be treated as individuals. Smaller groups enable you as the leader to focus on the names and needs of individual youth.
• Youth draw more personal identity from a small group as they get to know other students better. They also like to be able to identify who their teacher is.
• Adult teachers are more likely to be accountable for the youth enrolled in their small groups when they are with their assigned students from session to session.
• Small groups formed by gender often enable youth to be more honest about sensitive issues.

Usually, department time comes at the beginning of the session and includes welcome and recognitions, promotional announcements, prayer, and getting started into the Bible study. Yet, you could start in class or in special small-group teams during department time. A study that is more personal in nature could cause you to want to start and stay in class time for the entire session. A session that is more celebrative could be conducted in department time for the whole period. Your Youth Sunday School for a New Century leader guides will suggest a variety of approaches to grouping during a Bible study session.

You could also vary the way students go to small groups, whether classes or teams, during a session. Rather than send everyone to their permanent classes, you could divide them creatively into equal groups. Karen Dockrey, in her book, *Youth Worker's Guide to Creative Bible Study*,[3] identifies 32 ways to form teams or small groups. For example, beyond just numbering youth 1-2-3-4, consider using the last digits of phone numbers, birth months, birthdays within a month, favorite school subjects, hair color, eye color, favorite sports, puzzle pieces, and color of eyes.

Adding variety to how you group teenagers during the session will add life to your department. At the same time, though, being consistent in your grouping will add stability, deepen relationships, and increase accountability among adult leaders and youth. When there are no clearly defined class rolls or care groups, youth often "fall between the cracks" and get overlooked in ministry during the week and are sometimes treated as visitors when they come.

In addition to varying the grouping, the single best way every session to stay out of a rut is to vary your teaching-learning methods and approaches.

In the next chapter, we will examine closely eight teaching-learning approaches: relational, musical, logical, natural, physical, reflective, visual, and verbal. We will also look at principles for choosing which approach is best.

4. *Youth are introduced to a biblical truth that they continue to learn and live.*—For generations, we have called for youth to study their lessons prior to coming to Sunday School. Because Youth Sunday School Bible study groups are "open" every time they meet, beginning with resources released in the Fall of 2000, LifeWay Youth Sunday School materials assume the learners do not complete advanced preparation before the session. Instead, youth, whether they are already Christians or have never been to church, will be introduced to biblical truth that can

transform their lives. They will engage in study of the Bible text during the session. Then, they will continue focusing on the theme during the week to integrate the biblical truth into their lives using the learner guides and *essential connection*, the monthly devotional resource for youth.

In Family Bible Study the themes relate to all other age groups. Therefore, students may continue to explore the relevance of the biblical truth through family discussions. If the parents of your youth attend Adult Sunday School where Family Bible Study is used, their parents will be challenged to lead a "Family Bible Time" during the week where youth are given the opportunity to share what God's Word is teaching them. In addition, if a teenager's younger sibling (or even grandparents) are in Family Bible Study, the youth may initiate a question or conversation about what was studied. In addition, the pastor, minister of music, minister of youth, or other staff member may decide to fashion worship or other church events, such as Wednesday night worship and retreats, around the theme of Family Bible Study curriculum.

Family Bible Study has the subtitle of "Building the Family of Faith to Live by God's Truth." For youth whose parents are not in Sunday School or are not Christians, adult leaders and students become the spiritual family for that youth. In addition, both Family Bible Study and LifeTrak resources have parent newsletters that leaders can mail to parents informing them of what their teenagers are learning in Bible study. Finally, the youth has a take-home study sheet or page that he or she can use in personal study and perhaps share with their parents.

The 60-minute Bible study session is the beginning of transformational teaching. All leader guides provide a 60-minute teaching plan and reflect a common lesson format using *Prepare*, *Encounter*, and *Continue* segments. The teaching-learning experience extends to youth when they get home, go to school, or go to work. In addition, both adult leaders and youth leave the session realizing they are accountable to each other for what they do with that truth from session to session. Finally, Great Commission teachers recognize that they are not responsible for the results, only for faithfully involving students in understanding the message. Like Jesus in Luke 9:11, Great Commission teachers willingly accept "teachable moments" and engage in a "ministry of interruptions" during and after the session.

Endnotes

[1] According to a Kaiser Family Foundation study released on November 18, 1999, children younger than 8 years old spend an average of 5 hours and 29 minutes per day with media for recreation. Children older than 8 spend an average 6 hours and 43 minutes per day.

[2] Search Institute reported that 88 percent of youth workers believe that helping youth apply faith to daily decisions is "very important" but only 25 percent admit to doing it well. A 1997 LifeWay Youth Discipleship study of more than 2500 youth at summer conference centers indicates that one-fourth have considered suicide, three-fourths cannot control their temper, and half cheat on tests.

[3] Karen Dockrey, *The Youth Worker's Guide to Creative Bible Study*. Nashville: Broadman and Holman Publishers, 1999.

[4] Rick Yount, *Called to Teach*. Nashville: Broadman and Holman Publishers, 1999, 227.

[5] For general information about FAITH call toll free 1-877-324-8498.

What Works

At LifeWay Conference Center at Ridgecrest in July 1999, we asked youth leaders what was working in their Youth Sunday Schools. Here's some of what they said:

- Having youth from several cultures makes youth Sunday School exciting.
- Hands-on assignments.
- Students teach the class or team-teach with students or adults.
- Sharing testimonies about what God is doing.

New believers who share testimonies add "electricity".

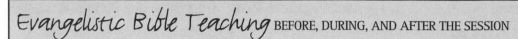

Evangelistic Bible Teaching BEFORE, DURING, AND AFTER THE SESSION

An enthusiastic ninth-grade Youth Sunday School leader called a LifeWay editor to say, "I know you don't get to hear about experiences like this very often, but I want to call to report that two youth accepted Christ during last Sunday's Bible study on heaven!"

Because Youth Sunday School Bible study groups are "open" to believers and non-believers, hopefully you, too, will be able to experience the joy of leading youth to pray to receive Christ. Rick Yount points out that Jesus had an unbeliever whom He taught for three years.[4] Jesus, however, accepted and embraced Judas and sought to teach him like the others. Like Jesus, youth teachers who teach evangelistically do so before, during, and after the session. Here are some suggestions:

BEFORE THE SESSION:
- Encourage your church to be evangelistic and be involved in its evangelism strategy. An evangelism strategy that increasing numbers of churches find effective is the FAITH Sunday School Evangelism Strategy.[5]
- Know the spiritual condition of youth on your roll.
- Learn to share your testimony and the plan of salvation in words youth understand.
- Be aware of lessons that relate readily to evangelism and find ways to tie any lesson to the plan of salvation. Note the places in the teaching plans that indicate evangelistic potential.
- Pray for lost youth by name.

DURING THE SESSION:
- Accept youth as they are and love them all!
- Use easy-to-understand words.
- Seek to create an atmosphere where all questions are welcome and wanted. Follow up questions with honest answers, including, "I don't know the answer to that question. I'll have to get back with you on that."
- Point out the plan of salvation feature in your learner guide or *essential connection* magazine.
- Be joyful and have a sense of humor.
- Help youth find Bible books and pronounce difficult words.
- Look for times to use your testimony of receiving Christ and for ways to involve Christian youth in sharing what faith in Christ means to them.
- Give youth the opportunity to pray to receive Christ during the session.

AFTER THE SESSION:
- Be available to youth immediately after the session or later in the week.
- Report to the minister of youth, pastor, or other church leader names of youth whom you believe need an evangelistic follow up.
- Volunteer to "walk the aisle" with a youth who wants to make a public profession of faith.
- Show youth the plan of salvation feature in your learner guide or *essential connection*.
- Seek to know, understand, and reach family members with the gospel.
- Use email and the Internet to follow up with lost youth.
- Make sure every new believer gets started in basic Christian discipleship, including baptism and daily time alone with God.

How Can We Best Encounter

GOD'S WORD IN A YOUTH BIBLE STUDY GROUP?

"Could I speak with you for a minute?" Kyle asked as he moved toward me. "I have a question."

I could tell that this Sunday's Bible study had struck home with the small group of seven high school guys—including a first-time visitor. At the beginning, we didn't agree on the best way to respond to a series of survey questions on marriage and divorce. The guys differed but they shared good reasons for what they said. Then we laughed together as we talked about some real-life situations. At the same time, I heard a number of honest questions and observed some serious Scripture searching. Then we read some "escape-clause" wedding vows and compared them to traditional wedding vows. When we looked in the learner guide, we found some specific implications for our lives based on what this passage said to us about present and future relationships, especially marriage.

As Kyle shared how he was struggling with applying the passage to a personal relationship, I realized that I had no quick solution to his struggle. He was dealing with what all maturing believers experience—living and obeying God's Word in daily relationships.

As we concluded the dialogue, he picked up a learner guide and asked, "Can I have this? I want to look at it some more."

"Yes, take it! In fact, I have something else I want to give you. Remember that you agreed to be one of the student leaders in our group? I have an extra leader guide that I want you to have. Would you be willing to help me lead a part of the Bible study session some time? If so, you'll need one of these books for teachers."

Kyle took it and smiled, "Yeah. And let's talk some more this week—by email."

What can you learn about leading a youth Bible study session from the preceding true story? Here are a few questions to help you reflect:

1. How would you describe the relationship between the class and the teacher? Between Kyle and the teacher?
2. What teaching methods were used? Why did they appear to be effective?
3. Recall the seven Bible teaching elements from chapter 4: *Acknowledge Authority, Search the Truth, Discover the Truth, Personalize the Truth, Struggle with the Truth, Believe the Truth,* and *Obey the Truth.* Which of the seven Bible teaching elements had Kyle experienced? How can you tell?
4. What resources were used during the Bible study session? What resources might be used after the session? How are these resources helpful?
5. Why did this Bible study connect to Kyle's life during the session? What do you think will happen after the session? Why?

In chapter 7 we explored what *encounter* means: *During the session, guide youth toward spiritual transformation through an encounter with God's Word in a Bible study group.* We learned that an effective Youth Sunday School Bible study group:

- Is "open" to believers and unbelievers and does not assume prior preparation by participants.
- Seeks to use all the time allotted to teach the "Biblical Truth" (total period teaching) and moves toward one or more proposed "Life Impact" statements.
- Has Bible study resources containing principles and terms that keep the leader and learners focused on Bible study.
- Has four characteristics: (1) Every student is loved and wanted. (2) The session flows so that leaders and learners remain focused on God's Word. (3) Youth are taught in a variety of ways. (4) Youth are introduced to a biblical truth that they continue to learn and live.

In this chapter, we'll examine how you can lead youth to *encounter* God's Word in the context of a Bible study group. Let's examine two Bible teaching strategies.

TWO BIBLE TEACHING STRATEGIES

The Bible is much more than a book of history. It has eternal truths and principles that we can relate to today's life issues and life questions. How do we understand these truths and communicate them? There are two different strategies, both of which can be found in the New Testament.

The first strategy is often called deductive, utilizing the process of thinking from the whole (such as a "Biblical Truth" statement) to the part (how people can apply this to life). From the Christian point of view, this strategy builds on the premise that God has spoken clearly in His Word and set forth truth for people to accept or reject. The Holy Spirit works through the teacher like a potter shaping clay. The concept of Bible storytelling—presenting the message of the Bible in historical narrative sequence—builds off of this strategy. The teacher's spiritual gift is to communicate effectively the biblical story and to ask questions to help create a learning climate for learners to engage the biblical truth.

Also called *direct instruction* or *expository teaching*, a pure deductive teaching-learning approach features:

- A teacher-centered point of view, placing more emphasis on teaching skills and the teacher's control of the pace, sequence, and content.
- Focus on mastery of content and learning objectives.
- Limited methodology, including discussion, lecture, question and answer.
- Convergent questions—usually requiring one correct answer.
- Resources that rely more on content through reading and securing information.

A second strategy is often called *inductive* and utilizes the process of thinking from the part to the whole. From the Christian point of view, this strategy builds

An effective Youth sunday school Bible study group is "open" to believers and unbelievers and does not assume prior preparation by participants.

on the premise that the Holy Spirit, the agent of spiritual transformation, leads learners to discover and interpret biblical truth for themselves through studying the Scriptures. God works through the teacher who acts like a gardener—cultivating the soil, planting seeds, and nurturing growth. The teacher-gardener then waits for fruit or understanding to emerge through the power of the Holy Spirit working in the believer. Through the Holy Spirit, each learner discovers the truths of the passage through personal study and participation in group interaction. The teacher's spiritual gift is to guide learners so they can discover personal biblical truths and help them apply biblical truth to their daily lives.

Also called *guided discovery*, a pure inductive model features:

- A learner-centered point of view, placing a balanced emphasis on teaching skills and learning skills with the teacher acting more as a facilitator of learning, guiding the pace, sequence, and content of instruction with learners.
- Focus on more complex thinking skills, such as analysis and synthesis.
- A variety of methodologies to match learning approaches and preferences, including problem-solving and group discussion.
- Divergent questions—encouraging many different responses. Inductive questions usually follow this pattern: (1) An approach question to introduce the lesson (ice breaker); (2) an observation question to discover the facts of the passage; (3) an interpretation question to discover the writer's basic meaning of the text; and (4) an application question to discover the personal, life-transforming message.
- Resources that reflect a more interactive format with responses to questions.

There is evidence that Jesus used both strategies. First, Jesus taught deductively when He sat in the synagogue, opened the Old Testament scroll, and declared, "Today this scripture is fulfilled in your hearing" (Luke 4:21). On the other hand, when Jesus told the parable of the sower in Matthew 13:1-17, He called for the disciples to discover for themselves the power of God's Word. When the disciples were slow to discern, He then led them step-by-step to understand the truth (Matt. 13:18-23).

Which strategy is best for helping youth experience the biblical process of instruction? The Holy Spirit can use either strategy or a combination of these teaching strategies effectively. Many teachers select elements from both teaching strategies to create a blended plan that is right for the group and most appropriate for the passage being studied. Such plans are built based on personal giftedness of the teacher, the content of the Bible passage, the size and setting of the group, and the preferred learning approaches of the participants. From session to session, the key is variety of methods. You will show youth how much you love them by teaching them in ways they learn best.

In chapter 6 we read about the variety of ways people learn and the eight learning-teaching approaches. Remember that methods are most effective when they address the teenagers' preferred learning approaches and developmental level. While the teacher usually chooses the methods, the learner could also select a method through which to study the Bible or experience the seven Bible teaching elements.

Rick Yount raises a good concern at this point, however. Learning is frequently hard and uncomfortable.[1] It's OK to stretch youth to move outside their preferred learning approaches. While youth find it easier to learn and their learning effectiveness increases when we use approaches in which they are already competent and comfortable, they also may build new competencies when we use activities that move them outside their "comfort zones." All of this is to say: Be sure to keep variety in your teaching plans so that all youth have opportunity to engage the Truth of God's Word in one or more ways they prefer.

ARE YOU TELLING A STORY?

An important skill to use with any method or within any approach is the ability to tell a good story. Jesus was a Master story teller. Parables make up as much as 30 percent of Jesus' teaching. His classic story of the Good Samaritan in Luke 10:25-37 involved His hearers in discovering, personalizing, and struggling with spiritual truth. The Bible, as much as 80 percent of which is narrative, is the true story of God's redemptive work throughout the centuries. The biblical pattern of telling the true stories of God's work from generation to generation can be found today in a variety of expressions beyond just lecture: drama, video, reading a poem, paraphrasing, interactive multimedia, or asking questions.

Telling a story helps youth move from the known to the unknown, from the concrete to the abstract.[2] True stories are often most captivating, as long as they are germane to the subject. Ways to make a story compelling include:
- using direct quotes;
- varying the intensity of the conflict in the story and saving the climax for the end;
- using pauses;
- appealing to the senses—especially visual;
- focusing on people; and
- using excitement, puzzlement, or concern.

QUESTIONS, QUESTIONS

Another skill to develop is the ability to ask a good question. Jesus asked many questions. He used questions to motivate His followers, awaken their conscience, call forth personal faith, rebuke criticism, introduce and follow up a story, compel thinking, or bring conviction. Following Jesus' example of asking good questions, we should:

- Move beyond fact-finding questions to open-ended questions. Avoid playing the game of "Twenty Questions" in which you ask questions that youth can answer only *yes* or *no* (or *God*, the standard "Sunday School" answer). Ask questions that call for youth to employ higher levels of thinking. For example, use words such as *describe, illustrate, rephrase, solve, conclude, interpret, compare, judge,* or *explain.*
- Keep questions simple and direct. A shorter question is usually more challenging. In Luke 9:20, Jesus asked, "But what about you? Who do you say I am?" (NIV)
- Ask questions that do not have to be or cannot be answered immediately. Think of the questions Jesus asked that were never answered! "What good is it," asked Jesus, "for a man to gain the whole world, and yet lose or forfeit his very self?" (Luke 9:25, NIV)
- Encourage questions from the youth themselves. Their questions are often the most thought-provoking and challenging!
- Use the awesome power of silence. Most teenagers can't stand silence! Give them time to struggle with your carefully crafted question. Avoid answering your own question by counting to 10 before you break the silence, by rephrasing or postponing the question to later in the session, or even until the next session.
- Allow youth to volunteer to answer questions. At the same time, give students who are more quiet opportunity to participate by directing questions evenly to all youth. You could help more reserved students by picking up on a conversation you had with them outside of the group setting.
- Be tactful in handling incorrect or inconsiderate responses by probing with a follow-up question or by redirecting the question to the group or to another person. In all things, communicate love to all students, not just to those who answer correctly.

"HELP! THERE ARE TOO MANY METHODS!"

You may be screaming at this point, wondering how you will ever choose the right teaching methods to use. Here are four principles to help you choose a variety of good teaching methods:

1. *Know your students.*—The information in chapters 2, 6, and 10 will help you understand how the age, developmental life issues, educational level, and family situations will help you choose methods that are on target. First, the writers and editors of LifeWay leader guides provide teaching-learning approaches that are appropriate for younger youth, older youth, or a combination of all youth. But, how do you find out the way your youth in particular like to learn? You could start by asking them. At the beginning of the Bible study year, ask students to complete a youth information sheet like the one provided in the appendix. Then, try out a variety of methods and see how youth react. In addition, pull aside one or two of your key youth, perhaps as student leaders, and ask them how they believe everyone is connecting with the Bible study. Better yet, involve students in helping you prepare and lead parts of the session.

2. *Know the nature of the Scripture passage.*—Choose approaches and methods appropriate for the passage. Some passages lend themselves to drama, especially narrative or gospel passages. Doctrinal passages, such as those in Romans, would lend themselves to reflective or logical approaches. The psalms are actually songs, and could be sung or paraphrased.

Allow yourself to occasionally try something radically creative with a passage. One teacher of seventh-grade boys brought a shovel to Sunday School to study Romans 6—an abstract passage about the death of the old life. He then took the guys outside the church building (*natural*), called upon them to record sinful attitudes and actions that Christ had "put to death" (*verbal*), and buried the attitudes with the shovel (*physical*).

3. *Consider the size and makeup of the group.*—Some approaches are best used in larger settings such as department time where you have more students. Drama, videos, and group singing are good examples. Other approaches are better used in small groups (class time) where relational, reflective, or logical approaches and methods are more effective.

Also, is the group made up of boys only? Is it coed? Is there a single culture or are there different cultures represented in the group? Cultural distinctives are important. For example, Rick Yount observes that Anglo-American and Asian-Eurocentric preferences for learning tend to be more task-oriented, whereas African-, Native-, and Mexican-American preferences tend to be more people-oriented.[4] At the same time, treat every person as an individual and never pre-judge.

4. *Know where you are in the flow of the session.*— Remember that you plan the session from "as youth arrive" to "when they leave." Begin with the end in mind as you choose the best teaching methods. For example, as you get started into the session, relational and musical approaches may "hook" the students' interest. You may seek to motivate them through giving them a problem to solve or controversial subject to debate. As you get into the truth of the Scriptures, logical approaches such as outlining the passage or visual approaches such as illustrating one or more truths may be more appropriate. Then as God's truth begins to get into minds and hearts, using a physical approach such as moving to an "agree" or "disagree" sign may solidify a decision in a teenager's mind about intended obedience.

Speaking of obedience, recall from chapter 3 that the goal of Great Commission teaching is obedience—spiritual transformation. The process of instruction includes

Try a variety of methods and see how your youth react.

seven Bible teaching elements that were introduced in chapter 4. Any of the eight learning approaches are appropriate for any of the seven Bible teaching elements. LifeWay Youth Sunday School leader guides will frequently identify not only the learning approach, but also the Bible teaching element that is dominant for a teaching-learning activity.

To help youth know the purpose of a particular activity, introduce the method with an explanation related to one of the seven Bible teaching elements. For example, say, "To help you struggle with this truth, let's look at this photo in your learner guide." Or "To personalize this biblical truth for today, read/listen to this testimony from a student in another part of the country."

USE THE BEST CURRICULUM RESOURCES

In chapter 4 we looked at principles for choosing sound curriculum plans. Now, let's look at choosing the best curriculum resources.

Make sure the resources you choose express the best curriculum plans. Sunday School for a New Century resources produced by LifeWay Christian Resources contain Bible study curriculum plans that are comprehensive, balanced, properly sequenced, and conducive to on-going ministry. These resources also address the five strategic principles for Sunday School ministry in the 21st century: foundational evangelism, foundational discipleship, family responsibility, spiritual transformation, and biblical leadership.

Teaching the Jesus Way: Building a Transformational Teaching Ministry lists eleven positive features of curriculum resources provided by LifeWay.

YOUTH FAMILY BIBLE STUDY RESOURCES

Family Bible Study resources are published quarterly for the Fall, Winter, Spring, and Summer seasons. A wide range of economically priced materials is provided for younger youth grades 7-8, older youth grades 9-12, and all youth grades 7-12.

Each age grouping has a learner guide, leader guide, and one or two leader packs. Class Packs and the All-Youth Leader Pack have CD-ROM's with music that can be played in CD players and files that can be opened and run on computers.

Because there are three distinctive groupings that Family Bible Study youth materials address, leaders have flexibility to mix and match the resources that are best for their church's organizational pattern and choose their preference of Bible translations. The all-youth learner guide comes in either KJV or NIV editions. The Scripture text is printed in all youth learner guides.

All learner guides are interactive and designed as tools for parents and teachers to engage youth in a meaningful and life-transforming study of God's Word during and after the session.

"Extra!" electronic teaching plan supplements are provided weekly on the Internet at www.lifeway.com or www.youthscape.com. *The Biblical Illustrator* is a supplemental resource for youth leaders that features additional Bible background and color photography and graphics on people, places, and events in the Bible study.

Family Bible Study instructional design and Bible study resources assume that youth do not complete advanced preparation before the session. Instead, each new lesson theme is introduced on Sunday. Youth are guided to engage in study of the Bible text during the session. Youth continue focusing on the theme during the week to integrate the Truth into their lives using both the learner guides and the devotional resource *essential connection* (*ec*), enhanced through family discussions. All leader guides provide a 60-minute teaching plan and reflect a common lesson format using *Prepare*, *Encounter*, and *Continue* segments.

Family Bible Study resources include a collection of supportive devotional resources for every family member that relates to the weekly common Bible study theme. For youth, the monthly magazine is titled *essential connection* (ec). Children have *More*, *Adventure*, and *Bible Express*, while adults have *Open Windows*. Family devotional elements are also included in selected adult learner guides.

LIFETRAK BIBLE STUDIES FOR YOUNGER YOUTH AND LIFETRAK BIBLE STUDIES FOR OLDER YOUTH

LifeTrak curriculum is an undated set of 13 Bible studies released quarterly that utilize a topic-driven Bible study plan distinctive to younger youth and older youth. *LifeTrak Bible Studies for Younger Youth* is actually a leader guide for younger youth, while *LifeTrak Bible Studies for Older Youth* is a leader guide for older youth. There are no learner guides, since each leader guide contains reproducible in-class handouts and take-home handouts. Both LifeTrak leader guides are based on the NIV. The Bible text is not printed.

The two separate leader guides enable churches of all sizes to address distinctive age group and generational life needs as appropriate to their unique situations.

LifeTrak instructional design and Bible study resources assume the learners do not complete advanced preparation before the session. Instead, each new Bible study is introduced in the session. Youth engage in study of the Bible text during the session using in-class reproducible handouts and then have take-home student sheets and an occasional parent newsletter to enhance family involvement with their youth in the study. All sessions provide a 60-minute teaching plan and reflect the common lesson format using *Prepare*, *Encounter*, and *Continue* and the seven Bible teaching-learning elements.

Separate devotionals for youth are found in *essential connection*.

ESSENTIALS FOR LIFE AFTER HIGH SCHOOL

Essentials for Life After High School is a set of 13 Bible studies to help high school seniors find biblical guidance to prepare them for life after high school.

Both a leader guide for the teacher and a learner guide for the students are available. Both utilize NIV, but do not print the Bible text.

Essentials for Life After High School instructional design and Bible study resources assume the learners do not complete advanced preparation before the session. Instead, each new lesson theme is introduced in the session. Students engage in study of the Bible text during the session using their own learner guide. They continue focusing on the Bible study to integrate the Truth into their lives following the session using the learner guide.

In the leader guide, all sessions provide a 60-minute teaching plan that is supplemented with multimedia slides on a floppy diskette. Students can also study the learner guide on their own if their church does not have a group study.

Separate devotionals for youth are found in *essential connection*.

WHY USE A LEARNER GUIDE?

To help youth get the most out of Bible teaching-learning before, during, and after the session, Sunday School leaders should take advantage of the most strategic tool other than the Bible itself—the learner guide. Learner guides for youth are designed to:

- provide youth with features on how to become a Christian and live for Christ. What other resource, week in and week out, better communicates the primary purpose of an "open" Bible study group than a well-designed learner's guide that prominently features the plan of salvation?

- help youth develop Bible knowledge and Christian convictions based on sound biblical exposition. Where else can youth learn more consistently what the Bible teaches on the Christian faith? In Bill Taylor's book, *21 Truths, Traditions, and Trends*, the author addresses the importance of a learner guide as a "constant monitor of doctrine."[5] He stresses that today's Sunday School learners are being bombarded with many varieties of false teachings and adds that many churches have almost abandoned leadership training for teachers, leaving teachers to teach tenets that could be detrimental to sound biblical doctrine. Learner guides provide the "true compass north" on biblical doctrine.
- encourage youth to develop life-long Bible study skills and Christian disciplines through providing Bible study helps. What better way is there to help youth learn to study the Bible, pray, and feed themselves spiritually on their own than through a well-designed learner guide?
- provide youth attractive visuals that engage them in reflective questions and biblical insights. How often do youth find photography and illustrations that beg them to examine and integrate God's Word?
- challenge youth to make a personal commitment to obey what God is teaching them. What tool will you provide after the session for God to use to reinforce the truths you teach on Sunday morning to help them to love, trust, and obey God in their daily lives?
- support a variety of learning approaches. When will youth who prefer to learn alone have their best opportunity to learn and obey the Scriptures?
- provide leaders with an economical tool for involving youth during the session for Bible research and response. How much does it cost in time and church resources to prepare or duplicate one-page handouts in comparison to multi-page full-color resources that are economically priced?
- assist youth in preparing for Bible study sessions. Where is the best place to introduce youth to the next session's Scripture and study?

To strengthen your Bible study experience, provide a learner guide for each Bible study participant, including visitors. Use the learner guide in the Bible study session as a tool for exploring the Bible passage. Show youth how to use the learner guide as a spiritual growth resource after the session. Finally, hold them accountable for obeying what God teaches from session to session.

LIFEWAY ONLINE AND CD-ROM RESOURCES

With every passing month, you will find more and more ways to utilize the Internet. Remember that *Extra!*, the electronic teaching supplement, is available every week for you to download free on www.lifeway.com or www.youthscape.com. You will also find the latest in free help for leadership development and other information on the interactive web site www.lifewaysundayschool.com. Since these web sites are dynamic, their content and features are continually improving. Bookmark these sites and check them often!

As you have read, there are CD-ROMs in selected Family Bible Study leader packs and LifeTrak volumes. On these CD-ROMs are a variety of electronic resources that can help you before, during, and after the session.

For before the session (*Prepare*), you'll find templates for plan sheets and teaching plans. You can customize these templates for your teaching plans. In some cases, you'll have additional commentary.

For during the session (*Encounter*), you will have presentation programs that you can run on a notebook computer or, if your church has projection equipment, project on a screen or wall. Contemporary songs to play or sing are also on these CD-ROMs and can be played on any CD player. Of course, you could put your teaching plan on your computer. One seventh-grade boys' teacher put his points on computer-generated slides and had the boys' rapt attention throughout the session. If you don't own a notebook computer, perhaps one of your students has access to one or a parent who owns one would participate with you in leading the session, at least from time to time.

For after the session (*Continue*), you'll find parent newsletters and other tips for continuing the ministry of teaching youth for spiritual transformation in daily life and family relationships.

OTHER TECHNOLOGIES

There are other ways to use technology in the 24/7 ministry of teaching youth the Bible. For example:

1. Use computer-based Bible study resources. You'll find there are available several editions of electronic study Bibles and reference resources, such as commentaries.

2. Access information from online Internet Service Providers (ISP). LifeWayonline.com is a new Internet Service Provider that filters objectionable material while giving you access to search for information that you can use to enrich your Bible studies. As already mentioned, be sure to get your weekly online teaching helps for Family Bible Study through www.lifeway.com.

3. Use desktop publishing and presentation software to create visuals, handouts, and multimedia for teaching. While you'll find such items in the CD-ROMs in Youth Sunday School for a New Century selected Family Bible Study packs and in LifeTrak volumes, you will also want to adapt or create your own. If you have a banner-making program, you could make banners using the "Biblical Truth" or even names of students for birthdays and announcements. You can also use presentation software programs to create your own visuals and slides for your lessons.

4. Create audio cassette tapes. While audio tapes are slowly being replaced by CDs, you can still use them to:

- Make recordings to help you and your youth memorize Scripture.
- Send an audio greeting from you or your class to a youth, especially one who is ill or who has moved. You could also record prayer concerns or make announcements.
- Listen to books on tape and share with youth.

5. Make and show videos. (Here's a great place where teenagers can get involved.) Show videos of youth involved in youth activities, dramatizing a Scripture passage, or making announcements.

6. Play recorded music or show video clips.

- Play contemporary Christian music or show contemporary Christian music videos as part of the "as youth arrive" or "when they leave" time.
- Play a song or show part of a music video with a listening sheet where youth record key words and phrases from the song or answers to questions that you discuss.
- Show movie clips or clips from TV shows to illustrate a key point in the Bible study. Remember, though, always to honor copyright laws. Make sure you show the clip in the context of a Bible study group at church. Showing a copyrighted video beyond educational fair use requires permission of the copyright owner. Also, model high standards in the movies or TV shows you show. Understand and communicate the underlying themes and messages of the media you are showing.

7. Use telephone answering machines and pagers.

- Leave encouraging messages to youth who aren't home when you call.
- Change your answering machine message to provide details of upcoming events for youth you think will call. You could also record a weekly greeting based on the lesson for that week.

Use desktop publishing and presentation software to create visuals, handouts, and multimedia for teaching.

- Check your answering machine and pager and respond to teenagers' messages promptly.
- Give pager numbers to parents when you take youth on trips so they can reach you in the event of an emergency.

8. Use cellular phones. They're everywhere!
- Use a cell phone to call for help when (not if) the bus breaks down!
- Use the phone to make appointments or get directions when visiting youth.

In general, be open to new technologies. Invest, though, in technologies only when their use will enhance your purpose of reaching and teaching youth. As you use technology, be sure not to lose the personal touch in your ministry. When building new facilities, try to anticipate technological needs with wiring, lighting, and focal wall placement.

Keep in mind that your youth are not afraid of technology, whether Internet, digital, video, audio, or a combination of them. Become familiar with the technologies your youth are using and then consider involving them in using the technologies as part of your 24/7 Bible teaching ministry.

SUGGESTIONS FOR THE MASTER TEACHER METHOD

The Master Teacher method revolves around one "master teacher" for a large group of teenagers. Other adult small-group leaders then debrief or help the students apply what the "master teacher" taught. The strength comes from having one teacher that is gifted at Bible study preparation and presentation. The other teachers or small group or family leaders study the lesson, but limit their teaching to application of the master teacher's presentation and ministry to students in the small group or "family" group.

Some churches choose to use a Master Teacher approach to Bible study in Youth Sunday School. Here are some helpful suggestions for how using LifeWay Youth Sunday School materials can work.

PRACTICE THE THREE ESSENTIALS: PREPARE, ENCOUNTER, CONTINUE

Every leader in Youth Sunday School, both the master teacher and the small group leader (sometimes called a care group leader, mentor, or family group leader), should be involved in all three of these essential parts of Youth Sunday School.
- Planning together helps define roles and responsibilities.
- Each leader grows spiritually as he or she *prepares* to lead youth to *encounter* God's Word through "Personal Bible Study" found in the leader guide.
- The Bible Study *encounter* should be focused on the "Biblical Truth" and the session should move leaders and learners toward transformation as suggested in the "Life Impact" statements listed in the leader guide.
- As each leader strives to be a genuine Christian example to youth, he or she participates in suggested *Continue* activities (after the session) found in the leader guide.

PRACTICE THE BIBLE TEACHING PROCESS
THAT LEADS TO SPIRITUAL TRANSFORMATION

As leaders become familiar with the Bible teaching elements, they may discover that some of the elements are more likely introduced in the learner's life by the master teacher, while other elements are introduced by small group leaders.
- The master teacher will likely lead youth to *Search the Truth* and *Discover the Truth* (these are more content-oriented steps).
- The small group leader will most likely focus youth on *Personalize the Truth*, *Struggle with the Truth*, and *Obey the Truth* (these usually are more application-oriented steps).
- All leaders will help youth *Acknowledge Authority* and *Obey the Truth*.

LEAD THE SESSION WITH A VARIETY OF
TEACHING-LEARNING METHODS AND APPROACHES

As you have learned, every teacher and leader should be aware that individuals learn in many different ways. LifeWay materials suggest eight approaches to teaching and learning with an unlimited number of teaching-learning methods. Using the leader guide as a starting place, every leader, master teacher, or small group leader can choose from a variety of teaching-learning approaches with youth.

First impressions when youth enter the room are critical. To create an "alive" ministry environment, vary the room arrangement, change posters or projected visuals, and change when and how announcements are made.

The master teacher should always avoid lecturing, and the small group leaders should avoid always using verbal discussion methods. For example, master teacher presentations should be supported with visuals, a listening sheet, multimedia, drama, or music. Small-group leaders should engage youth with a variety of learning approaches—including visuals, case studies, and study sheets. Constantly review and modify teaching plans while keeping a variety of teaching-learning approaches.

If a church doesn't have a qualified "master teacher" this approach becomes more difficult. Also when the master teacher is out for a Sunday or leaves the church, it may be difficult to find a capable new teacher. The master teacher's principle teaching method tends to be lecture while youth have a variety of learning styles and approaches. While small group leaders are easier to find, they may be less committed than class teachers who have accountability for both biblical instruction and ministry. Also because the master teacher is frequently teaching a wide age span, he or she may have a difficult time addressing specific needs common to all youth.

Whether you employ the master teacher approach or the teacher-class approach, do what is best for teenagers and not for the adults. The teacher-class approach may be challenging to keep staffed, but it is still the best method for most Sunday Schools because it builds from the adult Bible teacher's personal relationship with a small group of youth. Also, remember that every leader is the lesson in the sense that every adult—master teacher and small-group leader—is accountable for being an authentic example of the Christian life.

Endnotes

[1] William R. Yount, *Called to Teach*, Nashville: Broadman & Holman, 1999, 176.
[2] Ibid., 117-119.
[3] Yount, *Called to Teach*, 178
[4] Bill L. Taylor. *21 Truths, Traditions, and Trends.* Nashville: Convention Press, 1996, 158-159.

Always do what is best for the teenagers and not for the adults.

Twenty-first Century TEACHING TIPS THAT ENCOUNTER

- As you teach, keep in mind the "Biblical Truth" and "Life Impact" statements in your leader guide. Both serve as good boundaries for keeping your session flowing around God's Word.
- Review the "Options" for the teaching plan. Options call for additional preparation, but they have a higher level of creativity than the basic plan. Options may either supplement the activities or replace them.
- Give choices to youth for selected teaching-learning activities. Some youth may prefer to illustrate their response. Others may prefer to write or dramatize.
- Enhance your teaching through using leader packs, whether department or class packs. You will save preparation time, have attractive visuals, and find ready-made items for involving youth. In selected Family Bible Study leader packs and in all LifeTrak volumes, you will also find a CD-ROM with music you can play on any CD player along with presentation slides, customizable handouts, promotional handouts, audio files, parent helps, and other leader helps.
- If you use Family Bible Study, be sure to download the free "Extra!" files from www.lifeway.com or www. youthscape.com.
- While teaching the session, keep in mind your plan to extend teaching-learning to when they get home, go to school, or go to work.
- Follow your plan, but be sensitive to the Holy Spirit's leadership where God may take the group.
- Teach from the Bible and your notes or plan sheet. When directing youth to the Bible, give youth a reason to look into God's Word for themselves.
- To teach like Jesus taught, be passionate. "Listen carefully," Jesus implored in Luke 9:44. Emotion often drives how much attention a youth gives to learning. In turn, their attention influences how much they learn.
- To teach like Jesus taught, try to perceive what students are thinking (Luke 9:47). Try especially to connect with the student who doesn't seem to want to be there.
- To teach like Jesus taught, be willing to use object lessons (Luke 9:47-48).
- If you conduct a session outdoors, out of the church building, or on location, check with your church leaders about legal implications for transporting youth in your car.
- Vary how you use prayer during the session—sometimes at the beginning or in the middle as you respond spontaneously to students' concerns.
- As you go deeper into a biblical passage, be sensitive to students who are not versed in Scripture. Help youth locate Scriptures and explain terms clearly in words they understand. Remember that you are teaching an "open" group where you want kids present who don't know anything about the Bible.
- It's OK to leave students at the end of a session without having answered every question. Pledge that you will try to find the answers, but acknowledge that there are certain passages that we cannot understand completely to our satisfaction.
- Watch how kids respond to the hard teachings of Scripture. The youth who is open to the Lord will be drawn to God; the one who is looking for reasons to rebel will disobey the passages that are clear and be cynical about the passages that are difficult. Affirm youth for being honest about where they are with the Lord, yet encourage them to move on to love, trust, and obedience.
- Great Commission teachers utilize the value of organization (Luke 9:14). Enlist and equip student leaders to help you teach during the session and then evangelize, disciple, fellowship, minister, and worship after the session.
- Hold yourself accountable during the session. Do what you are asking your kids to do. Join with them in the teaching activity as often as practical.
- If you are using high tech equipment, get there early to make sure it works and is cued up.

CHAPTER 9

THE WHY? OF CONTINUING

Take a minute to recall the reporters that have been mentioned in this book. Imagine that one of them covers an event, writes the story, and the newspaper or magazine prints it. End of story–right? Not necessarily; sometimes a reporter keeps up with the people or circumstances to report on what happens next. Why would a reporter continue to follow a story? After a story has been published, what gives it staying power?

 Let's look at some of the blockbuster stories of this century: The bombing of Pearl Harbor, the assassination of President John F. Kennedy, the stock market crash of 1929 . . . even the tragic and premature death of Princess Diana. The stories were huge when they happened, but the continuation of each story proves the fascination of people to know what happened. A look backwards at Pearl Harbor (1941) includes revelations that a radar operator issued a warning that was unheeded; the conspiracy theories swirling around the investigation of the assassination of JFK have been a topic of conversation all the way into the new millennium; biographies of the richest persons in the United States at the time of the stock market crash reveal one bizarre occurrence after another. Beginning with a funeral service that was broadcast in the U.S. in the middle of the night, the saga of Princess Di has come around to trying to affix blame for her death on everyone from the driver to the press. There exists an almost insatiable desire to find new angles to old stories. *What is happening now? What are the subplots? Do we know the real story? Who are the characters? Who has been affected by the story? What has happened since?*

THE WHY? OF THE STORY

The story often lies in the *why* of what follows the original news item. The interest in the assassination of JFK remained in the myriad of stories that followed his death. America followed the life of Jackie Kennedy Onassis until she died a few

years ago. The picture of John Jr. saluting the funeral procession of his father became even more significant when John Jr. was killed in a plane crash in 1999. The *continue* of the story *is* the story!

Last summer at Lifeway Conference Center at Ridgecrest, North Carolina, my coauthor, Richard Barnes, said something that I cannot get out of my mind. He pointed out that our kids (pardon me, the young men and women that are in our classes) are, for the most part, very capable of making real-life connections between the biblical truths that are discussed and experienced during the *encounter* part of the lesson. His question to me was, "then why *don't* they?" Like many adults, youth are able to separate the cognitive application of the Scripture from it actually having any lasting impact on their lives.

Our conversation made me think about the teenagers whom we all know. I am thinking of those teenagers who seemed to have all of the right answers when they were in Sunday School; they went on the mission trips, and attended youth camp. Yet, as young adults, they are not now walking with the Lord. But let me tell you about a young man named Billy. Billy had a pretty rough hand dealt to him—his father left the family when Billy was two years old. His mother married and remarried, leaving her son to be raised largely by grandparents. Today, Billy is a youth minister with a tremendous ministry. He never wavered from his walk with the Lord. The *why?* of *continue* makes me wonder what happened with Billy that did not happen with the other teenagers. Why was his life transformed while the lives of some other youth apparently were not?

CONTINUE, CONT'D.

I feel like a stand-up comedian who says, "Stop me if you've heard this . . . ." Humor me, though; recall from chapter 4 that there are three essentials for teaching youth for spiritual transformation:
- Before the teaching session, *prepare* the ministry environment for spiritual transformation (chapters 1-4).
- During the session, guide youth toward spiritual transformation through an *encounter* with God's Word in a Bible study group (chapters 5-8).

- After the session, *continue* to guide youth toward spiritual transformation in daily living and family relationships (chapters 9-12).

Prepare is when we get ourselves and our teaching plan ready for the session. *Encounter* is when we introduce the *why* and *what* of a Scripture passage during a Bible study session. While we may discuss, write about, dramatize, or illustrate the "so what" of the Scriptures during the session, we and our learners will never truly value or understand the impact of God's Word until we connect its truth with everyday life experiences. Connecting with daily life is where *continue* enters the picture of teaching for spiritual transformation.

ONE MORE LOOK AT LUKE

In the preceding chapters, we looked at the ninth and tenth chapters of Luke to see the interaction between Jesus and those He taught. At the end of each "lesson" indications are that His hearers continued to do what they were taught. Some principles are suggested that may help explain the *why?* of continuing (italics added).

- For it to be most effective, continuing should begin immediately . Luke 9:6 says, "And departing, *they* began *going about among the villages, preaching the gospel, and healing everywhere.*"
- Continuing is most effective when accountability is initiated by the teacher. In Luke 9:10, the doctor writes, "And when the apostles returned, *they gave an account to Him of all that they had done.* And taking them with Him, He withdrew by Himself to a city called Bethsaida."
- Continuing requires a change in lifestyle, either a subtle adjustment or a radical redirection. Jesus gave instructions concerning the continuation of the lesson in Luke 9:23: "And He was saying to *them* all, "*If anyone wishes to come after Me, let him deny himself, and take up his cross daily, and follow Me.*"
- Continuing is not always completely understood until it is attempted. Occasionally, students can verbalize what continuing should consist of, but they really have no clue until they go out in faith. Jesus said in Luke 9:44-45: "*Let these words sink into your ears; for the Son of Man is going to be delivered into the hands of men.*" But they (the disciples) did not understand this statement, and it was concealed from them so that they might not perceive it; and they were afraid to ask Him about this statement.
- Continuing may seem easy, but it is possible to miss the commitment required. In Luke 9:61, the story is told of a student who thought he understood. "And another also said, "I will follow You, Lord; but first permit me to say good-bye to those at home." But Jesus said to him, '*No one, after putting his hand to the plow and looking back, is fit for the kingdom of God.*' "
- Continuing requires that hearers process the lesson and personalize the application and life change for themselves. In Luke 10:36-37, Jesus told the parable of the Good Samaritan. At the conclusion of the parable, He asked, "Which of these three do you think proved to be a neighbor to the man who fell into the robbers' *hands*?" And He said, "The one who showed mercy toward him." And Jesus said to him, "*Go and do the same.*"

CONTINUE ON, YOUNG TIMOTHY

A favorite Scripture of mine actually uses the word *continue* and captures the essence of what I am trying to say. Paul wrote to his young pastor friend to tell him that false teaching could not be allowed to grow. The apostle used words like *remember, guard, be strong,* and *commit* to identify tools to fight against the idle gossip (1 Tim. 5:13); the fables and endless genealogies (2 Tim. 4:4), the insistence

Continuing requires that hearers process the lesson and personalize the application and life change for themselves.

on legalistic lifestyles based on the denial of things (1 Tim. 4:3); and materialism (1 Tim. 6:9-10). Paul admonished Timothy not to be distracted, but to continue.

You, however, continue in the things you have learned and become convinced of, knowing from whom you have learned them; and that from childhood you have known the sacred writings which are able to give you the wisdom that leads to salvation through faith which is in Christ Jesus. All Scripture is inspired by God and profitable for teaching, for reproof, for correction, for training in righteousness; that the man of God may be adequate, equipped for every good work (2 Tim. 3:14-17).

The way to combat false teaching is to continue in the lessons you have learned. The protection against gossip or heresy becoming a part of your life is to allow Scripture to continue to instruct after the *encounter* is finished. According to the apostle, the *why?* of *continue* is to teach, reprove, correct, and equip the disciple.

THE "AMEN" THAT BEGINS THE WEEK

Transformation is teaching that lasts. Spiritual transformation is God's process of changing a life to love, trust, and obey God to His glory. While a teenager will be radically transformed—"born again"—through repentance and faith at a point in time (John 5:24), that same teenager must undergo the process of sanctification to grow in God's grace toward the goal of Christlikeness (2 Cor. 3:18). The lesson begins with a session, but it continues for a lifetime.

So, when you or one of your teenagers prays "Amen" at the end of the session, you have actually just begun the Bible study. You and your youth may not really struggle with the truth until you face a family conflict or an ethical dilemma. You may say you believe, but you won't prove it until you adjust your life to obey God's truth. And this usually means that God will test us to see how much we truly believe Him and His Word. Henry Blackaby called this a "crisis of belief."

Romans 12:2 states, "Do not conform any longer to the pattern of this world, but be transformed by the renewing of your mind. Then you will be able to test and approve what God's will is—his good, pleasing and perfect will."

The present passive imperative (*metamorphoumetha*) is used by Paul—to assure the reader that God Himself is at work—to change us into another form. Not just our outwardly visible appearance, but our character, our thinking, and our desires. Our very nature (essence) is reinvented when God transforms us. The image of this process presented by the prophet Jeremiah is of God as a potter who takes a lump of clay that had started to become one thing, wads it up in his giant, loving hands, and makes another piece that is perfect—according to His master design.

SPIRITUAL POP TESTS COME AFTER THE SESSION!

Throughout my years of education, I hated to go to a class where the teacher gave pop tests. I never knew exactly what to study and was anxious about when they were coming. I had to be ready every time I went to class. Now that I am a seminary professor, I still feel the same way about pop tests—only now I know that it is "more blessed to give than to receive!" (Just kidding.)

Spiritually, the timing of pop tests is different. Spiritual pop tests come after the Bible study session. As we (or our youth group) begin to internalize the truth of a lesson to the point that our lifestyles, relationships, habits, and behavior are altered, we should expect difficulties. Paul told Timothy, "And indeed, all who desire to live godly in Christ Jesus will be persecuted" (2 Tim 3:12).

Many of you can testify to the fact that once you learned a new biblical truth, you faced the "spiritual pop tests" that God allows. Scripture also witnesses to this truth. The apostle James made it clear that while God doesn't tempt us (Jas. 1:13),

Our very nature (essence) is reinvented when God transforms us.

He certainly allows trials to test our faith in the truth He teaches us. As a piece of pottery is made better by the fire, so we who face hardship as we *continue* are strengthened in the Lord:

Consider it pure joy, my brothers, whenever you face trials of many kinds, because you know that the testing of your faith develops perseverance. Perseverance must finish its work so that you may be mature and complete, not lacking anything. . . . Blessed is the man who perseveres under trial, because when he has stood the test, he will receive the crown of life that God has promised to those who love him. (Jas. 1:2-4,12)

Just a few sentences later James clarified that our obedience is the barometer that reveals whether we truly are learning God's Word:

Do not merely listen to the word, and so deceive yourselves. Do what it says. Anyone who listens to the word but does not do what it says is like a man who looks at his face in a mirror and, after looking at himself, goes away and immediately forgets what he looks like. But the man who looks intently into the perfect law that gives freedom, and continues to do this, not forgetting what he has heard, but doing it—he will be blessed in what he does. (Jas. 1:22-25)

Now, go back and circle the word *continues* in the passage above. Real application to life means that those who examine God's Word *continue* to remember and obey it. When we pass tests in real life through repentance, faith, and obedience, we are on the road toward maturity. The promise is that those who pass spiritual pop tests possess inner joy—"blessed" with God's favor!

A GOOD LESSON KEEPS ON TEACHING

The *why?* of *continue* means that the lesson suggests an action, provokes an emotion, or creates an image so powerful that the hearer thinks about the lesson as he or she goes through the week.

I received the following story via email and I think it is a great illustration of a lesson that actually resulted in changed behavior!

"According to a radio report, a middle school in Oregon was faced with a unique

problem. A number of girls were beginning to use lipstick and were putting it on in the bathroom at school. That was fine, but after they put on their lipstick they would press their lips to the mirror—leaving dozens of little lip prints.

"Finally the principal decided something had to be done. She called all the girls to the bathroom and met them there with the maintenance man. She explained that all the lip prints were causing a major problem for the custodian who had to clean the mirrors every night. To demonstrate how difficult it was to clean the mirrors, she asked the maintenance guy to clean one of the mirrors. He took out a long-handled squeegee, dipped it into the toilet and then cleaned the mirror.

"There have been no more lip prints on the mirror!"

WHY CONTINUE? BECAUSE IT IS THE WHOLE POINT!

Jesus' strategy of investing the future of the spread of the gospel in just 12 ordinary men is evidence that the *continue* part of the lesson is the pivotal aspect. The disciples not only heard and comprehended the teachings of the Master, the world was changed because they went on to live transformed lives (after an admittedly slow start!). If you're not yet convinced that part of learning God's ways includes real-life experiences that continue to teach and test us, reflect on Old Testament believers. Do you recall Abraham's test on Mount Moriah in Genesis 22? Or Gideon's desire for a sign in Judges 6? Or Jonah's one-way ticket? Exposure to God's truth calls for a change of mind that leads to faith, love, and obedience. The same is true in the New Testament:

- Matthew 7:24-29.—Jesus told the story of the two builders to illustrate that those who put His words into practice are wise and those who don't are foolish.
- John 8:31-32.—Jesus stressed that those who hold to (continue in) His teaching are real disciples who know truth and experience freedom.
- John 13:13-17.—Jesus washed His disciples' feet to give them the example to follow when they call Him, "Lord and Teacher," and then assured them of a blessing for obedience.
- Luke 24:13-35.—On the road to Emmaus, Jesus continued to teach from the Scriptures the same message of redemption.
- Colossians 2:6-7.—Receiving Christ as Lord is the beginning; continuing to live in Him "as you were taught" is when spiritual roots go down and spiritual building goes up.

Finally, think back on the *why?* of the reasons behind the writing of the letters in the New Testament that we call epistles. Were they not all written to *continue* teaching and instructing individuals and churches? They were meant to circulate among the churches so that they could all *continue* in the ways of the Lord. The *why?* behind continuing is the question that is answered as follows: Because if they don't follow, the chain of the gospel is broken. In a postmodern, post-churched world, *continuing* is an urgent task.

CHAPTER 10

WHO? Are the Youth We Teach?

THE OLD NEWSCAST JUST AIN'T WHAT IT USED TO BE

The TV evening news in your town is probably like mine. The local news hour has been downsized to thirty minutes. If you miss the news at 6:00 or 10:00, you can watch the "round the clock rebroadcast." Like a movie that runs continuously, your busy schedule can be accommodated by watching the news for any thirty-minute block you happen to have. Of course, if you are in the Eastern time zone, you probably watch the replay of the 6:00 newscast because you can't stay awake to see the end of the one at 11:00. (Remember the old days when you could make it through Letterman?) At one time, the entire 10:00 newscast used to be news. This is true no more.

I have done some research around the country (OK, I have stayed in a few hotel rooms!) and discovered that this phenomenon is not just in my hometown. In many cities, the newscast now includes a segment called "Consumer Watch" or "Buyer Beware." Here's how it works: A consumer feels ripped off by a company or service, so they call the hotline set up by the television station. The reporter places a call to follow up the initial report by the consumer who has been wronged. (It is best if the story is one that represents a typical complaint, meaning that several other people supposedly have been ripped off by the same company.) If the alleged ripoff would be emotionally appealing to the demographic profile of the audience who typically watches news on that particular station, the "on the spot" reporter pays the consumer a visit, accompanied by television production crews. Tears are shed in the interview and the reporter promises to get to the bottom of the problem.

Sometimes, the reporter shows up unannounced at the offending business to ask questions that have no right answer. Allegations are revealed, the company blames someone else, usually a subcontractor or a supplier of materials. The exposed and

embarrassed vendor pledges to make it right. Finally, the reporter looks sincerely at the camera and pledges to give us a report when the issue is resolved.

Several weeks later, the reporter follows up the story to show that things have changed in the lives of the person that was the subject of the interview—the *who?* Don't get me wrong—the action reporter does help the person. Most likely, he is driven by helpful motives. But the story is not in the fact that someone's toaster shorted out or that the home renovation company did not deliver on their promises. The story is in the *who?* The story is in how real people have to go on with their lives even after their fifteen minutes of fame. Remember the Larry Walters story in chapter 5? When the story was over, there was very little continuation. After he made his rounds of the talk shows, he was no longer the story. I would not speculate as to why he was in such despair that he would take his own life. I mean only that we as youth workers have to set the stage for the transformation that God intends for the lives of our teenagers—after the Bible study on Sunday. The story is the *who?*

BACK TO DR. LUKE

We have considered the ninth and tenth chapters of Luke as we have pondered the *why?* and *who?* of *prepare* and *encounter*. I'd like to put on my reporter hat and do some follow-up. Wouldn't it be cool to see how many of the five thousand who were fed physically and spiritually by Jesus were still around to see the resurrection? How many first-century Christian churches in Galilee had a person testify as to what Jesus did on that hillside that day? I wonder how many of the seventy evangelists became missionaries as the gospel began to spread throughout Asia minor? We know how the twelve turned out, but we can only speculate as to the others. The story is in the *who?* of *continue*.

In chapter 22, near the end of Luke's account of the life of Jesus, there is a remarkable story of a life transformed. On the night of the last supper, Jesus turned to Simon Peter and said to him, "Simon, Simon, behold, Satan has demanded *permission* to sift you like wheat; but I have prayed for you, that your faith may not fail; and you, when once you have turned again, strengthen your brothers," (Luke 22:31-32). The Lord was predicting the trials that were about to confront Simon. Jesus warned Peter that he would deny Him three times. Peter, of course denied the denial, emphatically stating that he was ready to die for Jesus.

Almost immediately after Jesus predicted that the rooster would signal the third and final denial, He was arrested and led to the house of Caiaphas, the high priest. There, Jesus was "questioned" which probably means tortured. While I was in Israel, I stood in the spot where it's believed that Peter warmed himself by a fire while he watched the mockery of a trial and three times denied Christ. Peter hit rock bottom. I was struck with the realization that I could deny Him as well.

You may remember "Top Gun"—a movie about jet fighter pilots in which the main character is a pilot nicknamed "Maverick," played by Tom Cruise. After losing his friend "Goose" in an accident, Maverick was reluctant to fly. There is a scene where the music builds when the battle desperately needs the skills of the grieving airman. The tide turns when Maverick's plane finally launches off of the deck of the carrier, starts to turn away, and then engages in the fight. After that momentous decision, of course, the "bogeys" were history.

If the life of Simon Peter was a movie, the music would probably build after the crucifixion of Jesus. Peter wept bitterly upon the realization that Jesus' prediction had come to pass (Luke 22:62). He continued to hang around the other disciples, and following the death and burial of Jesus, Peter was among the first to see that the tomb was empty on Easter morning. In John 21, Jesus appeared to Peter on the beach beside the Sea of Galilee to challenge him to feed the sheep. Only a few months later, in Luke's sequel to the gospel, we read of a different man.

And as they were speaking to the people, the priests and the captain of the temple guard, and the Sadducees, came upon them, being greatly disturbed because they were teaching the people and proclaiming in Jesus the resurrection from the dead. And they laid hands on them, and put them in jail until the next day, for it was already evening. But many of those who had heard the message believed; and the number of the men came to be about five thousand. And it came about on the next day, that their rulers and elders and scribes were gathered together in Jerusalem; and Annas the high priest was there, and Caiaphas and John and Alexander, and all who were of high-priestly descent. And when they had placed them in the center, they began to inquire, "By what power, or in what name, have you done this?" Then Peter, filled with the Holy Spirit, said to them, "Rulers and elders of the people, if we are on trial today for a benefit done to a sick man, as to how this man has been made well, let it be known to all of you, and to all the people of Israel, that by the name of Jesus Christ the Nazarene, whom you crucified, whom God raised from the dead– by this name this man stands here before you in good health. "He is the stone which was rejected by you, the builders, but which became the very corner stone. "And there is salvation in no one else; for there is no other name under heaven that has been given among men, by which we must be saved." Now as they observed the confidence of Peter and John, and understood that they were uneducated and untrained men, they were marveling, and began to recognize them as having been with Jesus (Acts 4:1-13).

Don't miss this: These men observed the confidence in Peter and John and concluded that the reason for their willingness to risk death for their testimony was that they had a relationship with Jesus. Transformed disciples, those teenagers who *continue,* may need to experience some of the same things that Peter did on his journey from Luke 22 to Acts 4. I shared a message on this topic for college students at Glorieta a few years ago. The question being considered in my sermon, was "What Caused the Change in Peter?" Consider a few of those experiences and draw your own conclusions.

• He remembered the words of Jesus (Luke 22:61): *And the Lord turned and looked at Peter. And Peter remembered the word of the Lord, how He had told him, "Before a cock crows today, you will deny Me three times."* In the Bible, we are told that we will struggle with being obedient to God. We may even be persecuted for the sake of Christ. Only by taking God's word into our hearts will adults and youth alike have a chance at holiness—and *continuing.*

• He wept tears of repentance over his failure (Luke 22:62): "And he went out and wept bitterly." When I speak to teenagers, sometimes I ask them how long it's been since they shed tears over the sin in their lives. It has become a great question for me as well. If I shrug off the fact that Jesus died for my forgiveness, I lose sight of how grieved God is over my sin. For the *who?* of *continue* to continue, they/we/I must grieve over sin.

• He continued to pursue Jesus (John 20:1-4): N*ow on the first day of the week Mary Magdalene came early to the tomb, while it was still dark, and saw the stone* already *taken away from the tomb. And so she ran and came to Simon Peter, and to the other disciple whom Jesus loved, and said to them, "They have taken* away *the Lord out of the tomb, and we do not know where they have laid Him." Peter therefore went forth, and the other disciple, and they were going to the tomb. And the two were running together; and the other disciple ran ahead faster than Peter,*

If I shrug off the fact that Jesus died for my forgiveness, I lose sight of how grieved God is over my sin.

and came to the tomb first. Too often, when we realize we have disappointed God, we stay away from Him. We quit having quiet times, we don't tell others about Him, and we even find other things to do rather than worship. How opposite from how He intended it to be as we continue in our walk with Him.

• He stayed still as he grieved over his sin (John 20). It is odd that we don't hear much from Peter in the early parts of this passage. Not until Peter is reunited with Jesus in the next chapter do we see his old talkative self. I am the champion of excuses. When I have messed up, I want to find someone to blame, someone to be mad at, someone to take away my guilt. Peter modeled that it is better to listen to God as He calls us back to Himself.

• He stayed around the other disciples (John 21:2): *There were together Simon Peter, and Thomas called Didymus, and Nathanael of Cana in Galilee, and the sons of Zebedee, and two others of His disciples.* If we don't want to face God, we surely don't want to face people who are His mouthpieces on earth. When I was a teenager and engaged in some experimental behavior with some of my nonchurched friends, I remember being offended when I, a reasonably active member of the youth group, was the recipient of a house call on youth visitation night. The explanation of my fantastic youth group was, "You should have been visiting with us and we wanted to make sure you were OK."

If a teenager remembers the Word because of our relationship and our teaching, comes to grip with the seriousness of his or her sin, remains with Jesus and His people, and continues to listen, that youth is on the way to joining Peter as part of the *who?* of *continuing.* I am encouraged because I can identify with Peter. He was a disciple who had a tough start, but went on to a strong finish. On the other hand, the list of those who failed to continue saddens me. What if Judas had understood that his ways were misguided? I know that he was fulfilling the prophetic words of Jesus, but he still had a choice. What if the rich young man who in Matthew 19:22, "went away grieved; for he was one who owned much property" had embraced the gospel rather than thinking the cost was too high? What if Nicodemus had been able to convince his fellow Pharisees that Jesus was the Messiah? If these lives, as well as those of some other people, had been transformed, and they had *continued,* we might be reading a very different Bible!

On a more local level, what about some of the students in your church? Some of them appear to be floundering, but with the right guidance, they will finish strong like Simon Peter. Others are weighing the truth of the gospel and counting the cost. A few of these will continue, and a few will consider the commitment to be too great. They will join the rich young man in an eternity away from Christ. Yes, fellow youth teacher, the stakes are high. Let's take a closer look at the *who?* of *continue,* and also at those students who choose to discontinue.

THE WHO? OF CONTINUE

The *who?* of continue are the students in your Bible study classes who are very bright, and for the most part spiritual-minded. They can explain what the Bible story has to do with life, but they still cheat in school, they still become involved in premarital sex, and they still struggle to remember to consistently model the kingdom lifestyle in their world. Glen Schultz, writing in *Youth Ministry Update*[1] cited some alarming statistics:

• In 1991, according to George Barna, only 53 percent of Bible-believing conservative Christians believe in absolute truth.

• In a 1997 seminar, Barna said that he believes that only 7 or 8 percent of today's Christians have a biblical understanding of life.

• Search Institute found in a survey of the mainline denominations (Southern Baptists included), that only 32 percent of church members believe that their faith has anything to do with life outside the church.

As mentioned in chapter 2, the world is getting much larger than it has ever been. The *who?* of *continue* could include teenagers from other backgrounds or religions who may have attended your class on any given Sunday. If a Jewish or Mormon teenager heard the gospel in your class, and God began to interpret its meaning in his or her life, the *continue* could include discussions in that family, as well as decisions about changing a lifelong way of thinking. The *who?* of *continue* is vitally important. (More on that after a brief detour to consider some kids who used to be around, but for some reason have disconnected.)

THE WHO? WHO DISCONTINUE

Unfortunately, the *who?* of continue also includes "who *doesn't* continue?" George Barna also reports that [research] "has consistently shown that between the ages of 18 and 24 we lose a very large percentage of young people who had been regulars at church."[2] Posted on the Barna Web site in January was more startling research. In an article entitled, "Teenagers Embrace Religion but Are Not Excited About Christianity," Barna wrote, "It is interesting to note that among those who deem themselves to be committed Christians, only half qualify as born-again Christians, a categorization that includes having 'made a personal commitment to Jesus Christ that is still important in [their] life today.' "

The Barna group questioned the youth in the study concerning the significance of spirituality as it relates to their future plans. The responses by the teenagers were not encouraging, scoring desirability of spiritual outcomes as moderate, at best. Barna continued, "Highest among the three religious-oriented outcomes was *having a close, personal relationship with God,* which ranked just eighth out of the nineteen possibilities. *Being deeply committed to the Christian faith* was in the bottom third of the future possibilities, ranked fourteenth. *Being personally active in a church* placed even lower—sixteenth. Overall, the highest-ranking options related to strong relationships and lifestyle comforts. Faith matters were substantially less compelling considerations."

According to the same study, while nearly nine out of ten teenagers "believe that Jesus was real, and more than eight out of ten describe themselves as Christian, only half say they are very eager to be deeply committed to the Christian faith. Even fewer—just four out of ten—are excited about being active in a church."

When asked to estimate the likelihood that they will continue to be involved in church in the future (despite incredibly high attendance patterns at present)[6], only one in three teenagers indicated they intend to be churchgoers after adolescence.

Herb Miller estimated that approximately 80% of young adults take a vacation from church between the ages of eighteen and twenty-seven.[7] He suggests six keys to keeping or re-engaging baby busters (birth years 1965-1983) in the local church. These keys may be easily adapted for millennials, the generation that follows the busters, and the generation in our youth ministries right now:

1. Baby busters must be in some leadership positions.
2. Church facilities and staff must be excellent.
3. The worship service (especially its music) must connect.
4. Small groups must be on the front line.
5. Churches may need to rethink organization built upon a hierarchical (pecking order) type of leadership.
6. The message must speak to the needs of real life.[8]

What is true for young adults is even more true for adolescents. Relatively few of them are coerced to go to church anymore. Even if our Sunday school lessons are *prepared* and *encountered* with utmost excellence, they will not *continue* if our attitude towards them and church is "you will grow into liking the way we do things." Youth must be able to participate in some church leadership. Their motivation to continue may be diminished if the youth department is in a rundown, poorly maintained part of the church, or if the leaders' attitude about worship is "youth preferences will pass, only hymns will last." For youth as well as young adults, small groups are preferable to large teaching groups. Because today's youth do not have the denominational loyalty of past generations, the need to connect them with church decision making and their continuation in church may go hand-in-hand. Keep in mind that continuation as transformed disciples and continuation as church members are not necessarily the same thing—but they are close. The reason that the writer of Hebrews in 10:24-26 told us not to quit meeting together is that we need the fellowship for stimulation for good deeds, for encouragement, for reminder of the Lord's return, and for rebuke and accountability with regard to sin. Continuation involves a fellowship of believers.

However, before you press the panic button, remember the portrait of the developing adolescent that you read in chapter 2. They are motivated by friendships more than institutions. Our job is to provide transformational teaching within the contexts of the relationships with peers and adults. Even though Barna's article was scary, it offered a voice of hope:

"Most teens are desperately striving to determine a valid and compelling purpose for life. Most of them want to have influence and impact. The Church has an opportunity to address such matters and thus to position itself as a place of valuable insight and assistance . . . . But to become an accepted partner in their maturation process, the Church must earn the time and attention of teens—and that means becoming a provider of value well before their high school graduation. The failure to do so virtually guarantees that the Church will continue to see massive dropout rates among college students, with relatively few of those young people returning to the church immediately after college."[9]

Only one in three teenagers indicated they intend to be churchgoers after adolescence.

EMOTION IN MOTION

Seven of ten youth attend church because they want to. In a survey conducted by Campus Life, the question was asked of teenagers, "Why do you go to church?" The main reason that youth attend church, according to the survey, is that (drumroll), "it helps them feel closer to God."[10] Feeling plays a huge role in the life of a teenager. For twenty years or so, we have been afraid of the role of emotion in education. Any decision that was made while in an emotional state was not considered valid. Perhaps we need to rethink.

In education, emotion is important because it drives attention[11] which jumpstarts learning and memory. In educational terms, we call the ability to recall facts *retention*. In dealing with spiritual truth, the goal does not stop with retention, but moves past to life change. In order for us to understand the *who?* of *continue*, we need to examine the part played by the emotions of an adolescent. Many decisions with long-term consequences are made on the basis of emotion. Emotion-induced behavior could include dating behavior, joining certain extracurricular clubs, or even behavior that is extremely destructive. The raw emotion revealed in the video tapes of Eric Harris and Dylan Kliebold shortly before they massacred students and a teacher at Columbine High School testifies to the power of feelings.

If the leader is to be the lesson, the emotions of the *who?* of *continue* cannot be underestimated. Reason may cancel out our emotions temporarily, but if our feelings are deep on an issue, they rarely change. Prejudice, anger, bitterness and pride are all emotions that affect the ability to learn. As you challenge your students to continue the lesson, you may find success as you use some teaching methods that bring emotion into the lesson. Asking questions without providing the answers, creating tension or surprise, even leaving a lesson "to be continued" until the next week—all bring in the element of emotion.

THE WHO? OF CONTINUE IS A LIMITED AUDIENCE

This is probably a good place to once again state the obvious. The only *who?* persons who can *continue* are the ones who have already been the recipients of the *prepare* and *encounter* under your competent leadership. The work of the Holy Spirit is not limited by my comprehension and I would not mean to exclude some people, but the parable of the soils seems appropriate (Mark 4:1-8). The only soils described were the ones who received seed of some kind. Soils that have not had any seed scattered on them are not eligible to have any type of growth on them. The only youth who will *continue* are the ones who have been reached through *prepare* and *encounter*.

THESE GUYS ARE GOOD

On a commercial for the PGA (professional golfers) tour, a fantastic shot is replayed and the announcer closes the ad by saying, "These guys are good." They *are* good, and when they are interviewed, they reveal why they're good. All of the golf stories have common ingredients:

- The men have natural talent.
- They were given an opportunity to learn golf at a young age.
- Someone took the time to teach them the game.
- They aren't afraid to try new shots (because they are confident they can build on what they already know).
- They spend an enormous amount of time practicing.

> The only youth who will continue are the ones who have been reached through prepare and encounter.

I was having a conversation with one of the young men in our youth group who was attending his university on a golf scholarship. After a few minutes he said, "Allen, I'd love to talk, but I have to go play eighteen holes with the team. We have to play every day to keep our scholarships." I recall being overcome with sadness that a young man would be forced to play golf every day just to stay in college; I suppose he has to learn sacrifice somewhere. (I'm kidding.)

The point is this: one way to discover and identify the *who?* of *continue* is to look at what those who are already continuing have done to get there. If I wanted to describe what it takes to continue as a golfer, I would examine the habits and lifestyle of Tiger Woods or David Duvall. If I want to understand a teenager who continues in a transformational lifestyle, I would examine some that have remained faithful over the years.

In seminary, I studied the work of a psychologist named Erik Erikson. I was intrigued by his work on adolescent identity primarily because his starting point was with young people who had healthy identities. Unlike some of the psychologists before him who studied sick people, he asked the question, "what makes a healthy person healthy?" A similar track was taken by the Search Institute in Minneapolis to examine the concept of success (we call it *continuing*) in teenagers today. Peter Benson's book, *What Makes Kids Succeed?* became an important work in my thinking.[12]

WHAT MAKES KIDS SUCCEED

Benson and his colleagues studied more than 250,000 teenagers in grades 6 through 12 in an attempt to identify what made "good" kids good. They initially identified thirty characteristics of successful teenagers and labeled them developmental assets. Explained on their Web page, Search Institute describes their work as follows:

"We're not talking about financial assets, but developmental assets—the "capital" children and youth need to grow up healthy, caring, and responsible. By examining extensive research on the influences in young peoples' lives, Search Institute has identified 40 developmental assets that form a foundation for healthy development. These are key factors that enhance the health and well-being of young people. If our society would invest more in the positive things young people need, then we could expect high yields (in terms of healthier youth) as young people become healthy, contributing members of families, communities, workplaces, and society."[13]

Like Youth Sunday School teachers identify the elements of a strength-based approach to healthy development, the 40 developmental assets (critical factors for young people's growth and development) make up a set of milemarkers for positive adolescent development. The concept of developmental assets also carries the assumption that the roles of families, schools, congregations, neighborhoods, youth organizations, and others are vital as influences in the lives of young people. The assets were described as coming from without (external assets) and within (internal assets). For convenience, I have included a list of both external and internal assets, some of which I have retitled for clarity. For further explanation, please refer to the Search Institute home page at www.search-institute.org.[14]

EXTERNAL ASSETS
- Family support
- Positive family communication
- Other adult relationships

- Caring neighborhood
- Caring school climate
- Parent involvement in schooling
- Perception that the community values youth
- Other youth as resources
- Service to others
- Safety
- Boundaries and expectations at home
- School boundaries
- Neighborhood boundaries
- Adult role models
- Positive peer influence
- High expectations
- Youth programs
- Religious community
- Time at home

INTERNAL ASSETS
- School engagement (motivated to involve self in school)
- Homework
- Bonding to school
- Reading for pleasure
- A positive value for caring
- Equality and social justice
- Integrity
- Honesty
- Responsibility
- Restraint
- Social competence in planning and decision making
- Interpersonal competence
- Cultural competence
- Resistance skills
- Peaceful conflict resolution
- Positive identity
- Personal power
- Self-esteem
- Sense of purpose
- Optimism about personal future

Positive and negative behaviors or outcomes were associated with the developmental assets proposed by Search Institute. Adolescents who have the positive assets in their lives are less likely to be involved in alcohol abuse, sexual promiscuity, and antisocial behavior. They are more likely to have healthy relationships with parents and peers and to make better grades. Such outcomes only make sense. However, we cannot look at the assets as a complete package. There are ways to place one or more of the internal or external assets into the lives of teenagers a little at a time so that gradually, they move toward even greater achievement. Success breeds success.

Please don't get bogged down in the lists. Remember that we are trying to describe the *who?* of *continue*. Who are the kids who keep on living out the words and Word of a Sunday School lesson long after the benediction in worship service has been spoken? When you eat at someone's home and they serve the most delicious

If I can only add one or two of those assets to teenagers in my Sunday school class, I will contribute to their success.

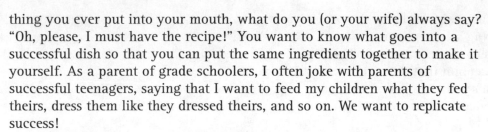

thing you ever put into your mouth, what do you (or your wife) always say? "Oh, please, I must have the recipe!" You want to know what goes into a successful dish so that you can put the same ingredients together to make it yourself. As a parent of grade schoolers, I often joke with parents of successful teenagers, saying that I want to feed my children what they fed theirs, dress them like they dressed theirs, and so on. We want to replicate success!

The problem is that the *who?* of continuing—that teenager that gets it and enters adulthood without a blip of wavering in their spiritual life—is both rare and unpredictable. As I process the developmental asset framework suggested by Search Institute, I come away thinking, *If I can only add one or two of those assets to teenagers in my Sunday School class, I will contribute to their success.* The same goes for the principles of transformational teaching. If, as a leader, I can be the lesson for one teenager, or if I can allow one teenager to struggle with the truth so they have to come up with the solution—if I can make the Scripture a life plan for only one or two youth, then maybe I am being faithful to the calling as an adult volunteer who works with youth.

In the next chapter, we will investigate the *what* of *continue*. As you are a leader and a lesson at the same time, never forget that God knows the *who?* teenagers better than anyone. He made them!

Endnotes

[1] Glen Schultz, "Why Teenagers Think as They Do" in *Youth Ministry Update*, Volume 10, Number 4, January 2000.

[2] Data presented at the Texas Baptist Youth Ministers; Conclave, October 31, 1999. Notes taken by the author.

[3] George Barna, "Teenagers Embrace Religion, but Are Not Excited About Christianity" posted on www.barna.org, January 11, 2000. These statistics were collected as part of a larger study of teenagers described in a new report by researcher George Barna entitled, "Third Millennium Teens."

[4] Ibid.

[5] Ibid.

[6]. The Barna group estimates that in a typical week, nearly six out of ten attend worship services; one out of three attend Sunday School; one out of three attend a youth group; and three out of ten participate in a small group other than a Sunday School class or youth group meeting. In total, more than seven out of ten teens are engaged in some church-related effort on a typical week. "Teenagers Embrace Religion, but Are Not Excited About Christianity" posted on www.barna.org, January 11, 2000.

[7] Herb Miller, "Demythologizing the Baby Buster Challenge," downloaded from www.churchresources.org, January 3, 2000.

[8] Ibid.

[9] Ibid.

[10] John C. LaRue, Jr., "What Teens Think About Church," originally published in *Youthviews*, the newsletter of the Gallup Youth Survey. Cited in *Your Church*, Volume 45, Number 3.

[11] Robert Sylvester, "How Emotions Affect Learning," *Educational Leadership* 52, 2:60-66.

[12] Benson, Peter, et al. *What Kids Need to Succeed*. Minneapolis: Free Spirit Press (Search Institute), 1995. This is a condensed version of a larger work entitled *The Troubled Journey: A Portrait of 6th-12th Grade Youth*, also by Benson and published by Search Institute, 1993.

[13] http://www.search-institute.org/

[14] Ibid, accessed January 15, 2000.

CHAPTER 11

What Does it Mean to Continue
TEACHING AFTER THE SESSION?

Monday, November 1
From: Kyle
To: Richard
Subject: <No subject>

*Hey Richard! It's been a long time since we last talked. I have a lot to tell you . . . .
I was gone from church because it was my dad's birthday, and my family and I went
out of town to be with my brother at college and to have some family time. It was a
fun day—I checked out an awesome Scripture last night, too. It was Ephesians 4:7-
14. It talked a lot about the role of a Christian and the role and importance of
pastors, evangelists, and pretty much every Christian. I was struck by the verse
directly following that one, which I think is about verse 11 or 12, when it said that
all of the people will mature to become servants to each other, and I just had a
revelation about how a pastor's job is to serve and a teacher is made to mature in
servanthood. I never really thought of it that way. Oh well, I just thought I would
share that with you. It really knocked me over last night. I hope to talk to you Wed.
night. Talk to you soon.*

By now you probably are getting used to the idea that teaching youth in Sunday
School is a seven-day-a-week strategy. Youth can get into God's Truth any day
during the week and you can lead them to do so at any time and in many ways. The
preceding email illustrates that Bible teaching and learning can take place even
when the teacher and youth are not present on the preceding Sunday!

Can we be intentional, though, to plan and seek ways to *continue* learning and teaching God's Word 24/7? How important is it to follow through with teenagers on what we teach during a session? How important is accountability for what we do with the truth from session to session?

WHERE CONTINUE FITS IN

Recall also from chapter 4 that we have identified seven Bible teaching elements that capture the way God seems to use His Word to transform lives:

- What authority, power, or rule guides my life related to this passage?—Acknowledge Authority (*control*)
- What did God say in the Scripture to the first readers or hearers?—Search the Truth (*content*)
- What abiding truth(s) for all generations is the Holy Spirit teaching from the Scriptures?—Discover the Truth (*concept*)
- Based on the abiding biblical truth(s), what is God teaching me about thinking, feeling, and living today?—Personalize the Truth (*context*)
- What conflict or crisis of belief is the Holy Spirit bringing about in my heart and life to challenge what I think and value and how I live?—Struggle with the Truth (*conflict*)
- How is the Holy Spirit leading me to live and repent—to change my mind, my values, or the way I live—or to resolve the conflict?—Believe the Truth (*conviction*)
- To what extent will I obey the Holy Spirit's leadership in what I think and value and the way I live?—Obey the Truth (*conduct*)

Examine the chart, "Three Essentials of Bible Teaching for Spiritual Transformation." (See Appendix.)

Note how *Struggle with the Truth*, *Believe the Truth*, and *Obey the Truth* overlap both the *Encounter* and *Continue* columns. You may have already concluded that most Bible study participants will not struggle with the truth of God's Word until after the Bible study session. The test for believing and obeying the truth will most likely come on a Monday morning or a Friday night—maybe even later in the month or year or lifetime!

At the same time, youth may not deal with the Bible teaching element of acknowledging the authority of who is truly calling the shots in their lives until they confront a real-life situation that demands a decision. Situations related to alcohol or other drug use or taking a public stand for Christ at an event such as "See You At the Pole" often cause teenagers to think about the lordship of Christ. Youth can also continue to search the Scriptures and discover biblical principles following the session, especially through Scripture memory, a learner guide, a family conversation, or a student take-home sheet. In short, any of the seven Bible teaching elements may be addressed during *Continue*.

Youth do learn biblical truth when they connect it to real-life activities, responsibilities, decisions, or dilemmas. Because Bible teaching that leads to spiritual transformation extends beyond the teaching session itself, *continue* means helping students connect their everyday experiences with the "Biblical Truth" they just studied in the session. Our goal is to get God's Word off the page and into the minds and hearts of the students.

A real-life illustration of *continue* occurred when Leah, a student leader of a high school mission trip group, accepted the responsibility to lead a devotional during mission trip training. As she began to share what God had laid on her heart, Leah used what she studied during that Sunday morning: the story of the Good Samaritan. Leah had searched, discovered, and personalized the truth to the

Our goal is to get God's Word off the page and into the minds and hearts of the students.

extent that she believed the truth enough to share with her peers. Later, as she actually went on the mission trip, Leah obeyed the truth by serving those in need.

CONTINUE THE TEACHING MINISTRY ANY WAY YOU CAN

Imagine for a moment that you have prepared and led a great Bible study session. Yet, because teaching Youth Sunday School is a strategy, not just a session, and teaching-learning doesn't stop when the session concludes, you start looking for ways to *continue* your teaching ministry 24 hours a day, seven days a week.

Much of what influences youth in Sunday School is beyond your control—the amount of support students receive in their families and the kind of acceptance and affirmation youth get from peers and at their schools. Nevertheless, you want to do all you can to help youth connect biblical truth with their family, friends, and school.

On the one hand, you recognize that you are not responsible for what students do with God's Word. After all, you can't make anyone believe and obey the Lord! Besides, Jesus Himself didn't force faith in Him. You are responsible, however, for faithfully involving students in understanding the message.

The most "teachable moments" usually lie outside the 60-minute block of time set aside for the Bible study session. And, like Jesus in Luke 9:11, you want to practice a "ministry of interruptions" before, during, and after the session to address questions, problems, needs, and issues as they arise in teenagers' lives. You realize that youth tend to adjust their beliefs and behavior—positively and negatively—by what they observe in others, including you!.

In the next chapter we will explore in detail how to *continue* teaching-learning. For now, though, determine to continue the teaching ministry wherever and however you can—at school activities, in conversation with parents and other family members, on church trips, by email, or in one-on-one times. Then consider expanding your teaching ministry to include youth from your Bible study group as student leaders to help you continue to teach. To help you get a feel for how you can *continue* teaching after the session, consider the following ideas:

- Send "encour-o-grams" (postcards, emails, or other notes of encouragement), reminding youth of the "Biblical Truth," Scripture passage, "Life Impact," or main biblical character.
- Mail a study sheet, handout, or take-home page to absentees and prospects with a personal note.
- Use ideas from "Questions, Questions" in chapter 8 or from the leader and learner guides to pose questions after the session in conversations, cards, letters, or emails.
- Point out to youth how the "Biblical Truth" relates to the larger biblical worldview categories of *Where did I/we come from?*, *How do I/we fit in?*, and *Where am I/we going?* (See the appendix for an overview of the Biblical Worldview that forms the framework for curriculum design for Sunday School for a New Century curriculum plans.)
- Point out a TV show, movie, recording, or Web site that relates to the previous session's Bible study. Ask youth for their opinion.

CONTINUE AND FAMILY RESPONSIBILITY

As you *continue* to teach, you will have opportunity to work with the families of youth. Sunday School affirms the home as the center of biblical guidance and helps equip Christian parents to fulfill their responsibilities as the primary Bible teachers and disciplers of their children. The major frontier for teaching youth in

God's Word is for all youth—whether they come to your classroom or not!

the 21st century is "family responsibility" through partnering with parents and other family members.

Obviously, the beginning point for you as the teacher is to get to know the parents of your youth. Learn their names and pray with them and for them. Tell parents what you are studying and ask them what they observe their teenager doing, if anything, with what you study during a Bible study session.

Biblically speaking, instruction through the home in partnership with God's people is the primary biblical model by which the Holy Spirit transforms lives (Prov. 22:6; Eph. 6:4; 2 Tim. 1:5-7). Integrating biblical truth into life is primarily the responsibility of the family as parents nurture their children in partnership with the church. Proverbs 4:1 extols the virtues of a "father's instruction." Learners, especially youth, have to cultivate a teachable spirit. In the Bible, especially the Old Testament, the largest number of teachers are the parents.

As we move to the New Testament, we see that the command in Ephesians 6:4 is specifically addressed to fathers, but it can apply to either parent. Parents should be equipping their children and youth to learn how to study and integrate God's Word into their own lives. As children mature and move into and through the teenage years, they become increasingly accountable for examining and integrating biblical truth into their own lives. Within the context of the home, parents can teach an apologetic of the Christian worldview to their children who are bombarded with many cultural worldviews. Any time a parent learns a new truth from God's Word in worship, Sunday School, or personal Bible study, he or she should ask, "How can I help my child/children understand, live, and obey this truth I have just learned?"

ACCOUNTABILITY FROM SESSION TO SESSION

Finally, one of the strategic principles of Sunday School for a New Century is Biblical Leadership. After the session, the leader is still the lesson. When you are allowing God's Word to transform you, you can teach from the overflow as you *continue* to live in your daily relationships.

Effective Sunday School leaders hold themselves, as well as the learners, accountable for obeying what God teaches from Sunday to Sunday. What if you and one or more youth came prepared to report on what God taught or how He used you in ministry since the previous Bible study session? What if you or the youth brought someone who needed to hear God's Word?

When students see that God's "abundant life" plan for them is spiritual transformation into Christlikeness, they will have a broad framework that the Holy Spirit can use to help them make sense of their day-to-day problems, questions, victories, and joys. Youth also want to make sense of what is happening with the larger picture of God, their friends, their family, their church, and their world. Because learning occurs all the time, some of the best learning and teaching times are spontaneous during the week. Helping youth be responsible to continue seeking God and learning God's Word after the session is the key to teaching that transforms lives 24/7.

In the Bible, especially the Old Testament, the largest number of teachers are the parents.

CHAPTER 12

How Do We Continue

TEACHING-LEARNING AFTER THE SESSION?

All week, I had tried to keep up with praying for my Sunday School guys'
concerns. On Saturday night, I felt compelled to call one of them.

"Hello, C.D.! How's it going? I hope you had a great week!"

"Not too bad, thanks. School's still there, you know. What's up with you? Why did
you call?"

"You remember last Sunday in Sunday School we had a prayer time at the end. I
wrote down your request for your grandmother. I'm calling to see how she's doing."

"Thanks for calling! I really appreciate your remembering to pray for her. Actually,
she seems to be doing a lot better now."

"That's an answer to our prayers!" I then reviewed what we studied last Sunday.
Just as I was about to say goodbye, C.D. asked, "What are we talking about
tomorrow?"

Admittedly, it's not every week a high school student asks what he or she is going
to study in Sunday School, but C.D. did. Based on what you read in the dialogue,
why do you think C.D. was interested in the next session's Bible study?

Because it is usually after the session when kids truly "get it," we must plan to
continue teaching beyond the session just as much as we plan to *encounter* God's Word
during the session. The time to start thinking about *continue* is when we *prepare*.

LifeWay Youth Sunday School for a New Century leader guides have a special
section for every teaching plan called *Continue*. There you will find several
continue ideas for every session. The ideas may range from books for further study
to prayer suggestions to ministry projects to referencing an article in *essential
connection*. The possibilities are virtually unlimited. You probably will use only one

idea each week, and you may want to adapt the idea to fit your group. Of course, you and your students could create your own, too. The duration of the activities is not limited to just the following week; some ideas may involve several weeks of planning and implementation. Some may even be classified as lifelong.

Whether you use an idea from the leader guide or create your own, almost every *continue* idea will probably relate to one or more of the following five *continue* strategies. Keep in mind that your purpose is to continue to guide youth after the session toward spiritual transformation in daily living and family relationships. With that as your goal, ask God to give you wisdom and energy to continue teaching youth anytime you have opportunity—night or day.

STRATEGY #1: BE WHO YOU ARE IN CHRIST!

At the conclusion of chapter 11, we stressed the fact that the strategic principle of Biblical Leadership affirms that the leader is still the lesson after the session, not just during the session. The first way to *continue* to teach after the session is to be who you are in Christ.

What motivates you as an adult to teach youth in Sunday School? Among many factors, hopefully you serve from a sense of God's call to love Him and to teach teenagers (Matt. 22:36-40).

But how do you deal with those times when you don't feel love for God or the youth? What do you do when you are struggling with whether you want to keep on teaching—especially after a session that bombs? Here's what you do: Focus on the Bible and not your feelings. Believe God's Word about who you are in Christ both as a believer and leader.[1]

There are many references in the New Testament to the position that believers have through faith in Christ. For example, John 15:1-5 states that as a believer, you are a living branch in the true vine. Christ will bear fruit through you. As a branch, you must remain in close fellowship with Jesus in order to continue to bear fruit, and you must allow the Father to bring discipline to your life to bear more fruit. Look at what you become as you remain in Christ—not just His servant, but His friend (John 15:15)! Now reflect on what Jesus said about you and the great promise about prayer in John 15:16: "You did not choose me, but I chose you and appointed you to go and bear fruit—fruit that will last. Then the Father will give you whatever you ask in my name." As you remain in Christ and discover you need something, ask the Father and then claim the promise that the answer is on the way! Remember, though, His answer will come in His time!

In Acts 1:8, Jesus assured us that the Holy Spirit empowers us to *be* witnesses, not *do* witnessing—being always comes before doing. Paul spelled out the relationship of being to teaching in Philippians 4:9, (NIV): "Whatever you have learned or received or heard from me, or seen in me—put it into practice. And the God of peace will be with you." Your youth will imitate the faith they see in you whether you invite them to or not. The question is not whether you will teach but whether you will be a good teacher—one worth imitating.

Here are four proven ways to remain in Christ.

1. Practice a daily time alone to read the Bible and pray. In *Youth Sunday School for a New Century*[2], Chuck Gartman offers this step-by-step approach to spending time alone with God:
- Pray. Ask God to meet with you and speak to you.
- Read from your Bible. You can follow a plan from a devotional guide as discussed below or divide the Sunday School Bible passage into daily portions.
- Write down what God is saying to you. Use a journal, such as the DiscipleHelps journal available from LifeWay.[2]
- Pray again, and record your prayer in your journal.

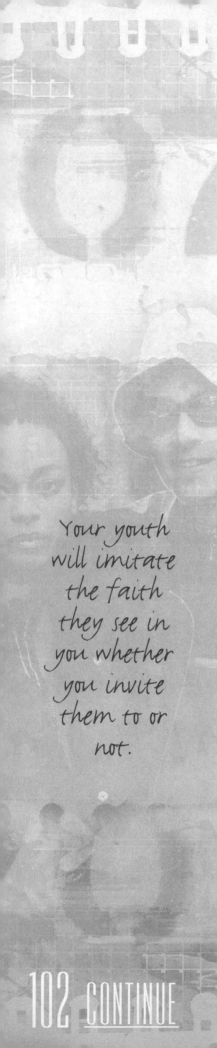

Your youth will imitate the faith they see in you whether you invite them to or not.

- Write an application statement. You could record a response to one or more of the seven Bible teaching elements introduced in chapter 4.
- Read a devotional thought. For Family Bible Study, the youth devotional guide, *essential connection*, has devotionals that *continue* the lesson Monday through Thursday. On Friday the devotional readings begin to focus on the upcoming study. If you use *ec* for your personal time alone with God, you will be continuing to live and learn the lessons you teach. If you use LifeTrak curriculum, you will still find *ec* to be a great way to connect with God every day. Plus, you'll get the benefit of trying to think from a youth's perspective. If you use a different daily devotional plan, consider using *ec* at some other point during the day, perhaps as an evening reading.
- Pray. Adore God by worshiping and praising Him. Confess attitudes or actions that He impresses upon your heart. Thank Him for forgiveness and answered prayer and then pray about your personal concerns and intercede for others. Keep a prayer list, perhaps organized by days of the week.

2. As often as possible every day, prepare a portion of the upcoming Bible study. Youth Family Bible Study leader guides have "Personal Bible Study" divided into three sections, one of which could be read on different days. Also, LifeTrak "Personal Bible Study" may be divided up to reflect on a smaller portion each day. In all youth materials, "Personal Bible Study" will guide you not only to be informed about God's Word but to be transformed by God's Word. The interactive questions, comments, and graphics will facilitate the Holy Spirit's work of transforming you to *be* the lesson, not just teach the lesson.
In addition, consider making the "Key Verse(s)" your personal memory verse every week. As you memorize and meditate upon key verses throughout the week, you will find how much God's Word transforms you and empowers you for teaching during and after the session.

3. Worship with others, including your family and your church family. All of the different age group Family Bible Study leader and learner guides have "Family

Bible Time" icons to identify places where the potential exists for family worship, discussions, or activities. Take a few moments at least once each week to share with other family members what you sense is God's message for you and your family. Such sharing could be done "as you go" when you drive children and teenagers to school or other places. You could also use age-group devotional guides, such as *essential connection*.

Then take advantage of corporate worship with your church family. Record worship notes on what God is saying to you through all aspects of the service from music to preaching. The DiscipleHelps journal has pages for worship notes. Then compare your notes with other believers and family members—especially the youth in your class or department.

4. Finally, enjoy who you are. Discover your spiritual gifts and use them. Develop your talents and hobbies. Be real. Protect your family time. Like Jesus, retreat when you're tired.

STRATEGY #2: TREACH!

When I served as youth minister in San Antonio, Texas, I lived near Theodore Roosevelt High School. Every time I drove by the school or went there, I noticed that the school logo connected the T and R. One day it dawned on me that that TR could symbolize what effective Youth Sunday School teachers do. Youth Sunday School teachers don't just teach; they TReach! That is, they teach with quality and reach with consistency. I immediately started using the word TReach to communicate to adult volunteers what I believe God wants us to do—teach and reach teenagers!

Make it your goal to touch the life of at least one youth or a youth's family member each week after the session. It's OK to blitz your whole roll occasionally with a card or email to everyone, but consistency week in and week out is more effective in the long run. Plus, it's often the simple, unexpected contact that a youth values the most.

You can see the youth at their home, school, job, recreation league, or anywhere. You might call or write them (email works!). Sending a postcard or email while you are out of town gets teenagers' attention. I knew an eighth-grade boy who loved the postcard of Texas A&M's Kyle Field that I mailed from Texas to Tennessee!

Help youth connect newly-learned truths with what they already know. One of the *continue* strategies I have used with students is asking them to record prayer concerns or praises on a three-by-five-inch card or half-sheet of paper. I then use these cards to guide my prayer time for students. I also use them in conversations and emails after the Sunday session.

When speaking to youth, consider questions such as:

1. What's going on with you these days? Listen carefully to what they say. (God has given us two ears and one mouth! Maybe we should listen twice as much as we talk—especially with teenagers.)
2. What would you like to know about our church or youth ministry?
3. (To those who were present): How has our last Bible study helped you this week? (To those who were absent): Here's what we are talking about in this week's Bible study.

If you see youth in person, offer them last session's study sheet, take-home page or handout, and/or the current issue of *essential connection* devotional guide. Show them the plan of salvation or features that relate to the week's Bible study. If you are writing them a letter, you could include the previous session's study sheet or handout with a personal note.

Youth Sunday school teachers don't just teach; they TReach!

If your dialogue focuses extensively on the Scripture passage from the previous session, ask or answer one or more of these questions:
- What command did God present?
- What promise did God make?
- What truth did God teach?
- What attitudes, beliefs, or behaviors will you make a part of your life?
- How does this Bible study affect your relationships with your family? With your friends? At school? With authority figures?

4. How is your family? (Ask for permission to report any crisis to your church staff.)
5. To those who haven't come in a long time, and in a spirit of humility,: How have we at the church or Sunday School let you down? How can we pray for you and your family?
6. May I tell you the greatest thing that has happened to me? In your personal opinion, what do you understand it takes for a person to go to heaven? (Then share your testimony and/or the plan of salvation from the learner guide or *ec*. Then leave the resource with them.)

If you are starting a new Sunday School year, you have 12 months to TReach everyone on your roll. If it is truly an open group, every class with 12 youth enrolled should seek to enroll at least one more youth after 12 months. That's TReaching!

Then, as you get deeper into the Sunday School year, add "Continue Strategy #3."

STRATEGY #3: INVOLVE STUDENT LEADERS

One clear trend in youth ministry in the last decade of the 20th century is the emergence of students as leaders in God's kingdom. Think about the impact of "See You at the Pole" and equal access campus Bible clubs. On U.S. public school campuses, if students do not lead "See You At the Pole" and campus clubs, they can't be done! Add "True Love Waits" and the growing volunteerism for missions, especially international missions, and you can see that this generation is taking personal responsibility for changing its world.

Go to any middle school and high school and see how often students are in the forefront of activity—from performing two hours of Shakespeare, to organizing a fund-raising campaign for a two-year-old with a brain tumor. Why shouldn't students who lead at school have opportunities to lead at church? All they need is adult encouragement and some organization, training, and resources.

One of the best places to start with youth is to gather them for prayer and vision-casting. When students get God's vision for what He is doing and wants to do, they will lead with creativity and passion. A good example of this occurred in 1999 after youth camp when students began a weekly prayer meeting. One prayer session was in August before school started when recent high school graduates were about to leave for college. A Youth Sunday School teacher suggested that the students divide into small groups and take a Youth Sunday School roll book and pray for every person on roll. As the book was passed around in my small group and students focused on each name, I sensed spiritual brokenness. I heard students pray earnestly for friends who were hurting, for those who were not coming, and for families who were struggling. When all the small groups came together for a final time of prayer, one recent graduate confessed that because she was going to college, she would probably never know whether people on her roll would ever come to Christ. With tears in her eyes, she challenged us, "Don't let this happen to you. Find these people and share Christ with them before you all graduate!"[3] A student shall lead them!

When students get God's vision for what He is doing and wants to do, they will lead with creativity and passion.

Share with the youth your vision for Sunday School and how it fits into the larger youth ministry and church. For starters, use the Sunday School definition found in the introduction to this book. Then list the five church functions of evangelism, discipleship, fellowship, ministry, and worship. Call for youth to lead in one of these functional areas. For example, enlist one youth to be the evangelism leader or organize an evangelism team. (Student FAITH teams function beautifully!) Then enlist a youth to be the discipleship leader for your class or department. In this role, the student serves as the student "link" to discipleship groups. They can also help to ensure each new believer gets a follow-up contact. Repeat this organizational strategy with the functions of fellowship, ministry, and worship. Remember that worship is both personal and corporate, and the worship leader could help lead a prayer chain of students in your class or department.

Another organizational approach consists of dividing the roll into smaller teams of both active and inactive youth within the class or department. Assign one or more youth as leaders for each team. Work with these student leaders to make sure everyone on roll over the period of the next 12 months is the recipient of the class's *continue* ministry.

The simplest strategy for involving students is to identify one student for every teacher to serve as a student leader for the class. The teacher then mentors and involves the student in the ministry of the small-group class. If you enlist only one student leader to help you with all five functions, consider rotating the students by quarter so that students don't burn out and other students get the opportunity to lead.

Part of leadership is accountability. One of the best ways to increase accountability on the part of all the youth is for you to build accountability into one or two student leaders. In your Youth Family Bible Study leader guide teaching plans, you will find suggestions for holding youth accountable for what was done in the previous session's Bible study. As you work with your student leaders, ask them to prepare to report from session to session.

From time to time, assign a student leader one or more parts of the lesson to lead in Bible study. Again, offer support and help to ensure that the student succeeds. Student leaders also can identify the issues with which youth are struggling.

Knowing these issues will help you focus the Bible study during the session and continue teaching and ministry after the session.

In addition, students can provide technical assistance with which many adults struggle. For example, students are often willing to put together media—creating a poster, making a video, sending emails, creating computer presentation slides, or running a multimedia presentation.

You can also work with students to plan fellowship or ministry activities with your class or department, especially those that continue the Bible study beyond the church's walls.

When working with student leaders, be clear on what you want them to do and then be available to advise and assist them. Don't hesitate to hold them accountable, but always look for ways to affirm them. You also will want to check with their parents to keep them informed.

Speaking of parents, we are now ready to consider our fourth *continue* strategy.

STRATEGY #4: MAKE CONTINUE A FAMILY AFFAIR

What do you think families expect of Youth Sunday School? In my experience, the most often-requested youth prayer concerns relate to family. I am convinced that Youth Sunday School must address family responsibility in practical ways. Could it be that the most neglected small group in the church is the family?

Perhaps we Sunday School leaders have inadvertently communicated that if parents brought (or even sent) their teenagers to Sunday School, we would teach them all they need to know about God. Yet, Deuteronomy 6:6-7 and other passages emphasize that the primary responsibility for spiritual instruction lies with parents, not the church. Therefore, Bible teaching sessions and the resources used before, during, and after the sessions should facilitate spiritual instruction within the family—at home, in the car, or wherever and whenever families are together. Sunday School exists for families, not families for Sunday School.

Building the curriculum plan with a common theme—preschool through adult— positions Family Bible Study to be family-friendly every Sunday. In addition, in every volume of LifeTrak curriculum there are parent newsletters for you to encourage parents and let them know what their youth is studying.

OK, teaching God's Word in and through the teenager's family sounds great, but how can we do it? Welcome to the frontier of family responsibility through Youth Sunday School! Addressing family responsibility is heightened when we *continue* teaching after the session. Here are some ideas to get you started into the journey of continuing Bible teaching and learning through families:

• Plan to encourage youth to share what they do in Sunday School with their family members. For example, in Family Bible Study point out the "Family Bible Time" icon to your students and suggest one or more ideas they could share with another family member, especially their parents.

• In *LifeTrak Bible Studies for Younger Youth* and *LifeTrak Bible Studies for Older Youth*, you will find a monthly newsletter that you can duplicate or customize and mail to parents of youth involved in your Bible study. You will also find parent newsletters on the CD-ROMs in selected Youth Family Bible Study leader packs.

• Consider setting a goal of personally contacting parents on a regular basis. You might set a goal of one parent per week or two per month. Point out that every week their youth will have a take-home study sheet that contains the "Family Bible Time" icon. You could mail an extra one to the parent. If you use LifeTrak, mail or deliver the monthly newsletter.

• Also, collect the email addresses of youth and parents in your class or small group and build an email list of both your students and their parents. Again, you'll find

Family
BIBLE TIME
DEUTERONOMY 6:7

electronic files that you can copy, paste, and email to parents in the CD-ROMs in selected Family Bible Study leader packs and on the CD-ROM in LifeTrak.

• Plan to order and distribute *essential connection* or *Living with Teenagers*. Both magazines can be great resources to help parents and youth. First, the monthly devotional guide for youth, *essential connection* (*ec*), could be used as a daily parent-youth devotional. *Living with Teenagers*[4] is also an excellent resource for parents to read. Parents will find helpful articles in every monthly issue.

• Provide help for parents to share the gospel and talk about spiritual matters with their teenagers. In the book *Family to Family*, Victor Lee and Jerry Pipes offer five suggestions to parents for sharing the gospel with their own teenagers. These five principles are sound for parents to use in any conversation with their teenagers, especially with regard to spiritual matters: (1) Have a platform of integrity and trust. (2) Have open communication. (3) Do not remove yourselves from the teenagers' culture. (4) Make it a point to talk with your teenager about salvation. (5) Be ready for any response.[5]

• As with youth, share your vision for Sunday School and how it fits into the larger youth ministry and church. Again, use the Sunday School definition in the introduction to this book for starters and share your vision for Youth Sunday School. Instead of asking parents how they can support you in Sunday School, ask parents to suggest ways Youth Sunday School can support them as a family.

• Plan fellowship or ministry events with your parents. Calendar one or more seminars just for parents of teenagers using the special parent edition of *Living with Teenagers*[4] or consider a parent, youth, and youth worker "trialogue" to discuss important family issues or plan youth ministry events. [6]

STRATEGY #5: BUILD ON THE FOUNDATION

Keep in mind that Sunday School is the "foundational strategy" for all other church ministries. As such, Youth Sunday School simply cannot do all that needs to be done in youth ministry. Most often, students will continue in other ministry and missions groups in the church. Youth may also continue the Bible study in campus clubs or other ministries outside your church. Regardless, support the adult leaders in other youth ministries groups by understanding what their ministry is, encouraging youth to get involved, and when possible, participating personally. For example, encourage youth to go deeper in:

• Student FAITH Sunday School Evangelism strategy[7] or the evangelism training your church offers.

• Discipleship groups, such as Experiencing God, Youth Edition, DiscipleLife Celebration, TM412, How Now Shall We Live? Student Edition,[8] or youth doctrine study groups.

• Mission trips and missions groups, such as Acteens, Youth on Mission, and Challengers.

• Mid-week youth worship. Building on the theme of Sunday School Bible study is a good strategy for *continuing* to teach.

• Special Bible study events, such as Youth Vacation Bible School, DiscipleNow weekends, or Youth January Bible Study, or weektime Bible studies.

• Music ministries, including youth choir and ensembles.

• Stewardship—as youth contribute their time, talents, and financial resources to the Lord's work through your church.

• Youth Ministry Council or youth lead teams.[6]

• "Equal access" campus clubs, campus missionaries, or other campus Christian organizations. Point out the "campus connection" Bible studies in the center of every monthly issue of *essential connection* magazine. These are written specifically for students to use when leading campus groups.

A PERSONAL WORD: "IT'S ALL ABOUT CHANGE"

Do you remember when you led your first youth Bible study group? I do. In 1969 I used a fill-in-the-blank Bible study on the Gospel of John that meant a lot to me when, as a high school senior, I accepted Christ.

Just a few years later—in the mid-1970s—I began writing Youth Sunday School and Discipleship materials for LifeWay (then The Baptist Sunday School Board). Then, in 1985, I moved to LifeWay to become professionally involved in publishing Youth Sunday School materials. I have personally tried many approaches to teaching youth—open classrooms, programmed learning, temporary study groups, reproducible handouts, simulation games, and all forms of multimedia. Teaching youth has been like trying to hit a moving target, and the target's still moving!

Besides the obvious explosion in Internet and multimedia technologies, what is different about teaching youth in the 21st century?

I believe the most profound change goes far beyond products, resources, and technologies, as helpful and necessary as these are. I believe the Lord is calling us anew to teach teenagers His unchanging Word so that their lives are changed to reflect Christ's character. I see a generation ready for nothing less than becoming like Him!

We were all moved by Cassie Bernall's bold affirmation, "Yes, I believe in God." Yet, as I listened on audio tape as Misty Bernall, Cassie's mother, read her book, *She Said Yes: The Unlikely Martyrdom of Cassie Bernall*, I was struck by Cassie's earlier testimony when she returned home from a youth retreat: "Mom, I've changed. I've totally changed. I know you are not going to believe it, but I'll prove it to you." Because Cassie had been so deeply involved in spiritual darkness, Misty admitted that she was skeptical. Yet, as time went by, Misty observed that Cassie had become a different person. "The important thing," Misty wrote, "was the change in her spirit—her gentleness, her humility, and her happiness. She seemed to have found a freedom she had never had before, and it changed the entire atmosphere in our house."[9]

In this book, Allen and I have attempted to articulate a strategy for teaching teenagers God's Word in such a way that the Holy Spirit can change their lives and

The gospel begins and ends with change . . . salvation in Christ changes our past, present, and future!

the lives of people around them. We believe three easy-to-remember words capture the essence of this strategy: *Prepare, Encounter,* and *Continue.*

Yet, we confess that, by themselves, strategies will not change lives. Personally, I have a renewed sense of dependence upon the Teacher, the Holy Spirit. I look forward to every youth Bible study session. To begin, I want God to use His Word to change me. Then I look forward to seeing how God uses His Word to change teenagers' lives, not just in the church classrooms, but in daily life and family relationships.

The gospel begins and ends with change. When Jesus first went public, He called for change: "The time has come. . . . The kingdom of God is near. Repent and believe the good news!" (Mark 1:15, NIV). Then we discover that His Kingdom is all about change. Salvation in Christ changes our past, present, and future: forgiveness from the penalty of past sins, freedom from the power of our sinful nature, and ultimate deliverance from the very presence of sin. These are changes I want this generation to know about! Don't you?

And we, who with unveiled faces all reflect the Lord's glory, are being transformed into his likeness with ever-increasing glory, which comes from the Lord, who is the Spirit.—2 Corinthians 3:18, NIV.

Dear friends, now we are children of God, and what we will be has not yet been made known. But we know that when he appears, we shall be like him, for we shall see him as he is.—1 John 3:2, NIV.

Listen, I tell you a mystery: We will not all sleep, but we will all be changed.—1 Corinthians 15:51, NIV.

Endnotes

[1] For an excellent study on discovering who you are in Christ, see *Jesus By Heart* by Roy Edgemon and Barry Sneed, Nashville: LifeWay Press, 1999.

[2] Available at LifeWay Christian Stores, www.lifewaystores.com, or by calling 1-800-458-2772 or www.lifeway.com/order/index.asp.

[3] In a Baptist Press release dated September 27, 1999, Thom Rainer of Southern Baptist Theological Seminary in Louisville, Kentucky, indicates that research shows that 83 percent of everyone who professed faith in Christ in this century did so before age 20, and 75 percent by age 14! As Youth Sunday School leaders, there must be an urgency to identifying and witnessing to lost youth on rolls before they graduate!

[4] Both *essential connection* and *Living with Teenagers* are available on the dated literature order form, by calling 1-800-458-2772, or on www.lifeway.com/order/index.asp.

[5] Lee, Victor and Jerry Pipes. *Family to Family, Families Making a Difference.* Alpharetta, GA: North American Mission Board, 1999, 48-49.

[6] An excellent resource for planning youth ministry that involves youth, youth workers, and parents is *Planning Youth Ministry from Boot Up to Exit* by Richard Ross, available at LifeWay Christian Stores, www.lifewaystores.com, or by calling 1-800-458-2772 or www.lifeway.com/order/index.asp.

[7] For general information about FAITH call toll free 1-877-324-8498 or see chapter 2, "Winning Youth at Home," in *Leading an Evangelistic Youth Ministry*, Richard Ross and Len Taylor, compilers, Nashville: LifeWay Press, 1999. *Leading an Evangelistic Youth Ministry* also has chapters on campus clubs, worship, youth ministry events, campus missionaries, streetwise youth, intercessory prayer, and mission projects.

[8] An excellent resource for teaching youth about worldview so they can learn that faith in Christ is a way of seeing, understanding, and changing their world is *How Now Shall We Live?* Student Edition by Chuck Colson and Nancy Pearcey, available at LifeWay Christian Stores, www.lifewaystores.com, or by calling 1-800-458-2772 or www.lifeway.com/order/index.asp.

[9] Misty Bernall, *She Said Yes: The Unlikely Martyrdom of Cassie Bernall.* Nashville: Word Publishing, 1999, 82-85.

Twenty-first Century TEACHING TIPS THAT CONTINUE

Where can you go to find ideas to *continue* teaching youth after the session?

1. Check your LifeWay Snday School for a New Century resources for *continue* ideas:

- Begin with the *Continue* section in your leader guide. Writers offer ideas from which you may choose. Usually, these ideas relate to one or more of the "Life Impact" statements found on the first page of the session. Don't hesitate to adapt the ideas to make them just right for your group.
- Also, check the unit pages in your leader guide. Some *continue* ideas are best accomplished over a period of weeks—or even longer.
- Look, too, at the Family Bible Study Leader Pack. You will not only find a printed resource you might use, but the CD-ROM in the class packs and all-youth leader pack often will have ideas that you can customize just for your Sunday School. The same will be true for the CD-ROM in LifeTrak volumes.
- The learner guide often has activities in the sessions or feature articles to which you can point youth for further study and response.
- Discipline yourself to memorize the "Key Verse(s)" for the week. You'll often find applications for using these verses in conversation and correspondence as you continue teaching.
- Note articles in *essential connection* and *Living with Teenagers* that you can share with youth and their families.

2. Check the Internet.

- Log on to www.lifeway.com or www.youthscape.com and download "Youth Extra!" for *continue* ideas. Also, continue to check www.lifewaysundayschool.com for the latest information on Sunday School for a New Century. There you'll find a weekly "Sunday School@Heart" article and a "Quick Tip" for every age group.
- The World Wide Web is ever changing. Here are some web sites that you may find helpful for *continue* ideas, especially related to family responsibility. LifeWay Youth Sunday School and hyperlinks to other Youth Ministries, such as Centrifuge, M-fuge, True Love Waits, World Changers, and "See You At the Pole."–www.youthscape.com
North American Mission Board Student Evangelism.–www.studentz.com
Acteens–www.acteens.com/acteens
Youth on Mission–www.wmu.com/wmu/organizations/youth
Ethics and Religious Liberty Commission of the SBC.–www.erlc.org
Center for Parent/Youth Understanding (Walt Mueller).–www.cpyu.org
Focus on the Family (James Dobson).–www.family.org

3. Create your own ideas.

- Share *continue* ideas with others during your leadership meeting.
- Write a letter or email when you need to communicate personally with a youth or parent.
- Create and use an email list of youth and/or their parents and send regular emails.
- Write a postcard to youth. It's possible that parents will see what you are saying. Here's one that I wrote: "Hi, Patti! I'm so glad you were a part of our Bible study on David and Jonathan last Sunday! You ask good questions! Guess what?! I found the verse about "a cup of cold water." It's Matthew 10:42. How are you coming on your friendship prescription? I sent a card and visited Brandon in the hospital. Please keep praying for him? C-U Sunday!"
- Either send a personal audiotape or tape your small group sending a greeting.
- Engage youth in on-line instant messaging via the Internet.

Appendix

Biblical Worldview Model

Family Bible Study: Understanding the Curriculum Design and Scope

Developmental Life Issues Charts

Youth Sunday School Plan Sheet

Approaches to Learning and Teaching for Youth

Youth Information Sheet

Three Essentials of Bible Teaching for Spiritual Transformation

Teaching Plan

Christian Growth Study Plan

* Permission is granted by LifeWay to reproduce any page of this appendix for use in church or conference leading.

BIBLICAL WORLDVIEW MODEL

Category	Universal Life Need	Representative Life Questions	Foundational Biblical Truth
			FUNDAMENTAL LIFE QUESTION: WHERE DID I/WE COME FROM?
Reason and Faith	To understand reality and knowledge	"What's real?" "Is there more to reality than meets the eye?" "How can I know that I know anything?" "Can I really know what I believe is true?"	Reality is fixed and knowable. Reality involves both material substance and non-material or spiritual substance. In other words, there is more to reality than meets the eye (Col 1:16). Much of what can be known is gained by reason, but faith lays hold of reality and knowledge that is not accessible to the senses (Heb. 11:1-3; 2 Tim. 1:12; Eph. 1:18; 2 Cor. 5:7; 1 Cor. 2:6-16).
The Person and Nature of God	To understand who or what has the power	"Who or what has the power?" "Is there a god?" "What is God like?"	Jehovah God is the only true God (2 Sam. 7:22; 1 Chron. 17:20; Isa. 44:6; 45:5-6,21). He is personal, all-powerful, sovereign (Ps. 115:3), transcendent (2 Chron. 6:18; Isa. 40:21-22; 55:8-9; Acts 17:24-25; Rev. 1:8), eternal (Gen.21:33; Deut. 32:40; 33:27; Neh. 9:5; Job 36:26; Ps. 90:1-2; 93:2 102:24-27; Isa. 40:28; 57:15; Jer. 10:10; Dan. 4:34; 1 Tim. 1:17; 6:16; Rev. 1:8; 4:8-9), unchanging (1 Sam. 15:29; Ps. 102:25-27; Mal. 3:6; Heb. 1:10-12; Jas. 1:17), and triune (Ex. 3:14; Gen.17:1; Dan. 5:21; John 10:30; Matt. 28:19; Acts 1:7-8; 2 Cor. 12:14). God is holy (Ex. 15:11; Ps. 99:9; Isa. 6:3; Lev. 11:44-45), just (Deut. 32:4; 2 Thess. 1:6), kind (Isa. 63:7; Jer. 9:24), good (Ps. 73:1; 1 Pet. 2:3), gracious (Ex. 22:27; Ps. 116:5; 2 Chron. 30:9; Joel 2:13), and loving (1 John 4:8). He is the creator of all that is, both visible and invisible (Gen. 1:1; Ps. 148:5; Isa. 40:26; Col. 1:16; Rev. 4:11). God is the source of all life (Acts 17:25). He acts out of love, grace, and compassion and desires the best for His creation (Jer. 29:11; Rom. 8:28; Eph. 1:11).
Creation	To understand origins	"Where did the world/we/my tribe come from?" "How did everything get started?" "What is the nature of the universe?"	Creation consists of both material or physical elements and immaterial or spiritual elements. God's creation functions with order, predictability, and splendor. God has established natural laws according to which the universe operates (Gen. 1:1; Col. 1:16; Gen. 8:21-22; Matt. 5:45).
Humanity	To understand identity and significance	"Who am/are I/we?" "Why am/are I/we here?" "Am/are I/we important?"	All people are created in the image of God and are, therefore, valuable as individuals. Human beings are total entities consisting of a material body and an immaterial spiritual part (Gen. 2:7; Eccl. 12:7). God made human beings male and female (Gen. 1:27). He gave them an equality of status but a difference of roles (Gen. 2:18). As the creation of a personal God, human beings possess personality, intellect, creativity, self-consciousness, and self-determination. Humanity's highest purpose is to love God and worship Him (Deut. 6:4; Ps. 96:9; Matt. 4:10; 22:37-38). Human beings are responsible to be good caretakers and stewards of God's creation (Gen. 1:28; 2:15). Even though everyone has fallen into sin and rebellion against God, through faith in Christ individuals can have their true humanity restored (Rom. 3:23; Eph. 4:24; Col. 3:10). Therefore the identity and significance of individuals is found in his or her being in the image of God by creation and by being in Christ by redemption (Gen. 1:27; 1 Cor. 15:22).
			FUNDAMENTAL LIFE QUESTION: HOW DO I/WE FIT IN?
Rebellion and Sin	To understand evil, suffering, and death	"What's wrong with the world?" "Why is there so much suffering in the world?" "Why do bad things happen to good people?" "Why do people die?" "Do evil forces exist?" "Why does evil exist?" "Why do I act the way I sometimes do?"	Rebellion of cosmic proportions has occurred in God's creation. Both spirit beings and human beings have rebelled against Him (Jude 6; Rom. 3:23). All human beings have sinned against God. Because all have sinned, everyone is fallen and lost. The relationship between God and every person has been broken. Sin has resulted in alienation, condemnation, enslavement, depravity, and death (Gen. 2:17; 3:19; Rom. 6:6; Eph. 4:18; Rom. 1:28; Titus 1:15; Rom. 6:23). Creation itself suffers from the impact of sin and is, therefore, no longer as God created it (Gen. 3:17-18; Rom. 8:22-23).

Category	Universal Life Need	Representative Life Questions	Foundational Biblical Truth
Sovereignty and Providence	To understand survival and security	"Do we live on a dying planet?" "What can we do to insure that the rain will fall and the crops will grow?" "How can I make it through the night?"	God is sovereign over His creation (Isa. 40:10, 12–17, 23–24; 45:9; Rom. 9:20–21). Nothing occurs without His permission (Job 1:12; 2:6; Acts 17:26; Rom. 8:28; Acts 2:23). God is at work in the world (John 5:17; Dan. 4:35; Ps. 135; Job 12:23; Ps. 22:28; 66:7; Matt. 6:8; 1 Sam. 2:6–7). He actively continues to preserve (Isa. 40:26; Neh. 9:6; Ps. 36:6; Col. 1:17; Isa. 40:11), provide for (Matt. 6:25–34; Ps. 104), and sustain His creation (Heb. 1:3; Job 34:14–15). He providentially controls, guides, and directs the universe and history toward His desired end, in spite of all hindrances (Gen. 50:20; Dan. 4:34–35; Ps. 135:6; Prov. 16:4,33; Rom. 5:6; Rom. 8:38–39; Eph. 1:9–11). God preserves the stability and order of the natural realm through natural laws (Gen. 1:14; 8:22; Job 37:6–13; 38:1–41; Ps. 135:5–7; Ps. 104; Jer. 31:35; Matt. 5:45). God works through His natural laws to renew His creation's resources and to meet the on-going needs of humanity (Ex. 23:10–12; Lev. 25:1–7, 18–22; 26:34–35; 2 Chron. 7:13–14; Ps. 104:30; Ezek. 36:1–12, 28–30, 33–36). God preserves the stability and order of the social realm through the bonds of marriage and family (Matt. 19:2–8; 1 Pet. 2:13–17; Titus 3:1), and stable civil government (Dan. 2:21; 1 Pet. 2:13–17; Titus 3:1).
Revelation and Authority	To understand truth and assurance	"What is truth?" "Is something true just because those in charge say it is?" "What should I/we believe?" "How can I/we know what's true when there are so many competing voices?" "Whom can I/we trust?" "What's important and what's not?"	God has revealed Himself in many ways—through nature, conscience, and special acts, including Scripture and Jesus Christ (Rom. 1:18–20; Ps. 19:1–4; Rom. 2:14–15; Heb. 1:1–2). God has spoken objectively, personally, and propositionally. His revelation is intelligent and intelligible, true and trustworthy, authoritative and final (2 Tim. 3:16; 2 Pet. 1:20–21; Mark 13:31). Because it is God who has spoken in the words of the Bible, the Bible is authoritative in all that it affirms, teaches, and commands (John 10:35; Ps. 119:105; 19:7–11). Hence the Bible has the authority to command our beliefs and order our behavior (Matt. 22:29; 2 Tim. 3:17; Deut. 11:18–19).
Ethics and Morality	To understand actions and behavior	"What's right and what's wrong?" "Is there a standard by which all people should live?" "How can I be good?" "What should I/we do?"	God is a holy God. He is the moral standard by which all moral judgments are measured (1 Pet. 1:15–16; Isa. 5:20–21; Mal. 2:17). God created human beings with a moral nature and has established moral absolutes (Ex. 20:1–17). As such, humans are moral agents who are morally responsible to God. Human beings have both personal and social moral obligations (Eph. 5:22—6:9; Rom. 13:1–7). God has revealed His moral standards through human conscience, Scripture, and the witness of the Holy Spirit. Human beings, therefore, are responsible for abiding by creation ethics and Christian ethics (Rom. 14:12; 1 Pet. 4:1–7; Rev. 20:11–15; 2 Pet. 3:11–12,14).
Covenant and Redemption	To understand renewal and restoration	"Is there any way I can start over again?" "Is there any way I can make up for or undo past mistakes?" "Can I be delivered from the bondage I experience?" "How can I overcome feelings of alienation and estrangement?" "How can I be forgiven?" "How can I be saved?"	God was not thwarted by the rebellion of His creation. He has chosen to call into being a covenant people whom He blesses and restores (Gen. 12:1–3; Ex. 6:1–8; Eph. 3:10; Rev. 5:9; 14:6). God initiated this blessing under the old covenant and will fulfill it under His new covenant, which was inaugurated by Jesus Christ (Jer. 31:31–34; Luke 22:19–20). God's covenant is an act of divine grace and calls for fidelity on the part of His people (2 Tim. 2:11–13; Matt. 25:23; 1 Cor. 4:2; 1 Pet. 1:13–14). God has acted in history to redeem human beings and His creation through His Son, Jesus Christ. In Jesus Christ, God entered into time and space in human form, and He suffered and died to atone for sin in the place of (as a substitute for) human beings (John 1:14; Phil. 2:6–8; Mark 10:45; 1 Tim. 2:6; Rom. 5:8; Acts 13:38; Eph. 1:7; Col. 1:14). This is the basis of the hope of redemption. God offers forgiveness of sins and reconciliation to those who will trust in Christ's sacrifice (Rom. 5:10–11). To them, God promises hope, resurrection, and victory (Acts 24:15; Titus 3:7; 1 Thess. 5:8; Col. 1:27; 1 Cor. 15:42–57).

Category	Universal Life Need	Representative Life Questions	Foundational Biblical Truth
Family, Community, Church, and Kingdom	Love and a sense of belonging	"Does anyone care about me?" "How come nobody loves me?" "Is there a place I can feel completely accepted and at home?"	God made people to need other people (Gen. 2:18-23). God ordained the family (Gen. 2:23-24; Ex. 20:12; Matt. 19:3-6), communities, societies, and nations (Rom. 13:1-2; Isa. 45:1; Acts 17:26; Prov. 8:15; Dan. 2:21,37; 4:17; 5:18-21) to accomplish His purposes in our lives through love, discipline, encouragement, and security (Heb. 12:7-11; Deut. 4:9-10; Prov. 31; Rom. 13:1-7; Eph. 6:1-9; Col. 3:18--4:1; 1 Tim. 3:4-5,12; Titus 3:1; 1 Pet. 2:13-17). Believers discover their purpose and identity in relationship to their families, the people of God, the fellowship of Christ's church, and the realm of His kingdom (Matt. 5:16; 12:49-50; Mark 10:28-30; 1 John 3:1-2; John 15:13-16; Eph. 2:11-22; 1 Cor. 12:12-31; Matt. 24:42-47; Matt. 6:33).
Discipleship and the Christian Life	To understand fulfillment	"Who shall I/we be?" "How can I/we be acceptable?" "How can I/we be important?" "How can I/we be great?" "How can I/we find fulfillment?"	Believers achieve greatness through being transformed into the image of Jesus Christ and by giving themselves to His service and ministry (Matt. 23:11; 1 Pet. 4:10-11). The Christian life is a life of discipleship that involves self-denial (Matt. 16:24), obedience to God's commands (John 14:15,21; 1 John. 5:2-3), vigilance in prayer (1 Thess. 5:17), an authentic witness (Matt. 28:16-20; Acts 1:8), cultivation of the mind of Christ (Phil. 2:5), production of the fruit of the Spirit (Gal. 5:22-23), progression in holiness (2 Pet. 3:18; 2 Cor. 3:18; Phil. 1:6; Col. 3:9-10; 2 Tim. 2:22; Phil. 2:12-13; 1 Pet. 2:2; Rom. 12:1-2), demonstration of Christian virtues (2 Pet. 1:5-9; Phil. 4:8; Col. 3:12-14), and perseverance in faithfulness (Phil. 1:6; 2 Tim. 2:19; 2 Pet. 2:20; 1 Cor. 9:27). Growth in Christ is characterized by an awareness of the positional nature of redemption and the completed work of Christ in the life of the believer (1 John. 3:1; Eph. 2:6; Col. 1:27).

FUNDAMENTAL LIFE QUESTION: WHERE AM I/WE GOING?

Category	Universal Life Need	Representative Life Questions	Foundational Biblical Truth
Time and Eternity	To understand history's meaning, direction, and purpose	"Where are we going?" "Is there hope for something better than this?" "Are history and the universe heading toward a goal or is it all meaningless?" "Is this all there is?" "What happens to me when I die?" "Is there life after death?" "Do you only go around once?"	God is not limited by time (Ex. 3:13-15; Ps. 90:2-4; 102:24-27; Isa. 41:4; 44:6; 46:9-10; 48:12; 57:15; 1 Tim. 1:17; Heb. 13:8; 2 Pet. 3:8-9; Rev. 1:8; 15:3; 21:6; 22:13). He works within time to accomplish His purposes (Gen. 50:20; Ps. 135:6; Dan. 2:21; 4:34-35; Prov. 16:33; John 10:10; Rom. 5:6; Gal. 4:4-7; Eph. 1:3-14; 3:2-11; 1 Tim. 6:15; Titus 2:11-14; Heb. 1:1-2; 2:9-10). The Bible presents a progressive view of time (Acts 1:7; 24:25; 17:26). Time is moving forward meaningfully and purposely because God is moving time, history, and creation toward a determined end (Ps. 33:11; Acts 3:18-21; Rom. 8:28-30, 38-39; Eph. 1:3-14). Someday Jesus will return in power and great glory (Matt. 16:27; 24:30; 25:30-31; Mark 13:26; 14:62; Luke 9:26; 21:27; 1 Thess. 4:16; 2 Thess. 1:8; Titus 2:13; Rev. 19:11-21) to raise the dead (Dan. 12:2; John 5:25, 28-29; Acts 24:14-15; 1 Cor. 15:51-52; 1 Thess. 4:13-16), judge the world (Matt. 16:27; 25:31-46; Acts 17:30-31; Rom. 2:5; 14:9-12; 1 Cor. 4:5; 2 Cor. 5:10; 2 Thess. 1:7-10; 2 Tim. 4:1; Rev. 20:11-15), punish the lost in a place called hell (Matt. 8:12; 25:41,46; 2 Thess. 1:8-9; 2 Tim. 4:1; 1 Pet. 1:4-5), reward the redeemed in heaven (John 14:2-3; 1 Thess. 4:17; 1 Pet. 1:4-5), establish His kingdom (Dan. 2:34-35, 44-45; Matt. 6:10; Luke 22:28-30; 2 Tim. 4:1; Rev. 11:15; 20:1-6), renew heaven and earth (Rom. 8:19-21; Heb. 1:11-12; 12:26-27; 2 Pet. 3:10-13; Rev. 21:1-27), and consummate His redemptive mission (Acts 3:20; Eph. 1:9-10; Phil. 2:10-11; 1 Cor. 15:24-28; Heb. 9:27-28).

UNDERSTANDING THE CURRICULUM DESIGN AND SCOPE

BIBLE STUDY APPROACH

Family Bible Study reflects a curriculum plan designed to achieve the goal of "Building the Family of Faith to Live by God's Truth." This Bible study plan provides a common Bible study theme each week for the five Sunday School divisions—preschool, children, youth, young adults, adults—with common Bible passages for all ages as often as suitable.

Bible Study Content Design

Family Bible Study uses a comprehensive, balanced, and appropriately sequenced study of Bible books, people, doctrine, history, and classic Bible passages. The content is organized around biblical worldview questions (such as: Who am I? Who is God? Why am I here?) and addresses life issues.

Note the following three attachments:
● An overview of the biblical worldview model, which is used as a tool to balance the content of the Bible studies (attachment A)
● An explanation of the Scope content categories
● A chart that pairs biblical worldview categories with fundamental life needs. (The fundamental life needs represent human needs that all humans share, whether or not they articulate those needs. These fundamental needs are the foundation for developing life issues which are expressed in the context and culture of the learners.)

BIBLICAL WORLDVIEW MODEL (an overview)

Plot:
The flow of history is about the longings and actions of a loving, gracious God who created all things for His purposes, acted in history to redeem His fallen creation through Christ Jesus, and promises to someday restore His redeemed creation.

Prologue
Fundamental Life Question: Where did I/we come from?

Fundamental Biblical Answer: According to the Bible, Jehovah God created all things with purpose, and He created all people in His image.

Biblical Worldview Categories:
● God
● Faith and reason
● Creation
● Humanity

Story
Fundamental Life Question: Where and how do I/we fit in?

Fundamental Biblical Answer: The Bible teaches that although everyone has sinned and rebelled against God, He graciously offers forgiveness, restoration, purpose, and community through His Son Jesus Christ.

Biblical Worldview Categories:
● Rebellion and Sin
● Covenant and Redemption
● Family, Community, and Church
● Sovereignty and Providence
● Revelation and Authority
● Ethics and Morality
● Discipleship

Epilogue
Fundamental Life Question: Where am I/are we going?

Fundamental Biblical Answer: The Scriptures promise that through Christ's salvation, God is present and active both now and forever in those who receive Him.

Biblical Worldview Category:
● Time and Eternity

The Scope of Family Bible Study

Bible content categories represent "scope" areas. For Sunday School resources, the scope of study is the Bible; the entire Bible. But to claim the entire Bible as a single scope category is far too broad for meaningful curriculum planning. This model focuses on five scope (Bible content) categories for guiding study plan development.

1. **Bible Books.** The original, intended message of the Bible book.

2. **Bible Characters.** Individuals or groups who played a recorded role in the biblical revelation.

3. **Themes.** Major themes occurring in the Bible such as salvation, faith, grace, obedience, and so forth.

4. **Bible Story.** The plot, eras, and events which frame the historical context for the Divine Revelation.

5. **Bible Teachings.** Passages or books with a fairly specific didactic purpose. Examples could include the Sermon on the Mount, the Ten Commandments, Paul's writings to the churches, prophetic sermons, and so forth.

The above designations should not be perceived merely as approaches or types of Bible studies, though they may parallel a variety of different kinds of studies. The intent is to reflect the divine pattern of objective, recorded revelation. In order to encompass the full scope of the Bible, we must understand how God has spoken to us through the written Word. In the Bible, God chose to speak through recurring themes. God chose to speak through real events in history. God chose to speak through the lives of real people in real life. He chose to speak through authors who recorded unique and varied messages from a variety of times and places. God chose to speak through very specific, recorded teachings which are intended to convey timeless principles and absolutes. The categories above reflect the divine pattern.

ELEMENTS OF A BIBLICAL WORLDVIEW

Fundamental Life Need	Foundational Biblical Worldview Category
1. To live consistently with a correct understanding of **reality** and **knowledge**	**Reason and Faith**
2. To live consistently with a correct understanding of **power**	**God**
3. To live consistently with a correct understanding of the **origins** of the universe	**Creation**
4. To live consistently with a correct understanding of personal **identity** and **significance**	**Humanity**
5. To live consistently with a correct understanding of **evil, suffering,** and **death**	**Rebellion and Sin**
6. To live with a plausible confidence that I will **survive** and be **secure (survival and security)**	**Sovereignty and Providence**
7. To live with a correct understanding of **truth (truth and assurance)**	**Revelation and Authority**
8. To live with a correct understanding of how I should **act** and **behave (actions and behavior)**	**Ethics and Morality**
9. To live with a plausible hope of **renewal** and **restoration**	**Covenant and Redemption**
10. To live with a plausible sense of **love** and **belonging**	**Community, Church, and Kingdom**
11. To live with a plausible **hope** of **fulfillment (lifestyle and fulfillment)**	**Discipleship and the Christian Life**
12. To live with a correct understanding of **history's meaning, direction,** and **purpose**	**Time and Eternity**

DEVELOPMENTAL LIFE ISSUES CHART LIFETRAK CURRICULUM—YOUNGER YOUTH

Type of Learning	Developmental Life Issue	Primary Worldview Category	Life Question
Know (Cognitive)	1. Hope	Sovereignty and Providence	Where am I going?
	2. New Life in Christ	Covenant and Redemption	Where am I going?
	3. Heaven	Time and Eternity	Where am I going?
	4. Creation	Creation	Where did I come from?
	5. Assurance	Covenant and Redemption	How do I fit in?
	6. Family	Family, Community, and Church	How do I fit in?
	7. Sanctity of Life	Humanity	How do I fit in?
	8. Church	Family Community, and Church	Where do I come from?
	9. God	God	Where did I come from?
	10. Absolutes	Revelation and Authority	How do I fit in?
Be (Affective)	11. Health	Humanity	How do I fit in?
	12. Values	Ethics and Morality	How do I fit in?
	13. Self-Esteem	Humanity	How do I fit in?
	14. Gender Development	Humanity	How do I fit in?
	15. Freedom in Christ	Covenant and Redemption	Where am I going?
	16. Encouragement	Family, Community, and Church	How do I fit in?
	17. Trust	Family, Community, and Church	How do I fit in?
	18. Honesty	Ethics and Morality	How do I fit in?
	19. Obedience	Ethics and Morality	How do I fit in?
	20. Gratitude	Discipleship	How do I fit in?
Do (Behavioral)	21. Relationships	Family, Community, and Church	How do I fit in?
	22. Fellowship	Family, Community, and Church	How do I fit in?
	23. Ministry	Family, Community, and Church	Where am I going?
	24. God's Word	Revelation and Authority	How do I fit in?
	25. Communication	Family, Community, and Church	How do I fit in?
	26. Worship	Covenant and Redemption	How do I fit in?
	27. Dealing with Sin	Rebellion and Sin	How do I fit in?
	28. Influence	Family, Community, and Church	Where am I going?
	29. Stress Management	Sovereignty and Providence	How do I fit in?
	30. Prayer	Covenant and Redemption	How do I fit in?

TOWARD SPIRITUAL TRANSFORMATION (JAMES 1:22, JOHN 14:15)

DEVELOPMENTAL LIFE ISSUES CHART LIFETRAK CURRICULUM—OLDER YOUTH

Type of Learning	Developmental Life Issue	Primary Worldview Category	Life Question
Know (Cognitive)	1. Worldview	Faith and Reason	Where did I come from?
	2. Spiritual Gifts	Humanity	How do I fit in?
	3. Vocation	Discipleship	Where am I going?
	4. Spiritual Transformation	Discipleship	Where am I going?
	5. Forgiveness	Covenant and Redemption	How do I fit in?
	6. Suffering	Rebellion and Sin	How do I fit in?
	7. Facing Death	Time and Eternity	Where am I going?
	8. Truth	Revelation and Authority	Where did I come from?
	9. The Holy Spirit	God	How do I fit in?
	10. Peace	Sovereignty and Providence	How do I fit in?
Be (Affective)	11. Ethics	Ethics and Morality	How do I fit in?
	12. Priorities	Time and Eternity	How do I fit in?
	13. Purity	Ethics and Morality	How do I fit in?
	14. Integrity	Ethics and Morality	How do I fit in?
	15. Discernment	Revelation and Authority	Where am I going?
	16. Teachability	Discipleship	Where am I going?
	17. Honor	Ethics and Morality	How do I fit in?
	18. Authority	Revelation and Authority	How do I fit in?
	19. Justice	Ethics and Morality	Where am I going?
	20. Service	Family, Community, and Church	Where am I going?
Do (Behavioral)	21. Christian Dating	Family, Community, and Church	Where am I going?
	22. Stewardship	Humanity	Where am I going?
	23. Missions	Discipleship	Where am I going?
	24. Leadership	Discipleship	Where am I going?
	25. Relating to Family	Family, Community, and Church	How do I fit in?
	26. Impact	Family, Community, and Church	Where am I going?
	27. Relationships	Family, Community, and church	How do I fit in?
	28. Evangelism	Discipleship	Where am I going?
	29. Worship	Covenant and Redemption	How do I fit in?
	30. Scripture	Revelation and Authority	How do I fit in?

TOWARD SPIRITUAL TRANSFORMATION (JAMES 1:22, JOHN 14:15)

YOUTH SUNDAY SCHOOL PLAN SHEET

YOUTH SUNDAY SCHOOL PLAN SHEET

RESOURCES NEEDED/ PERSONS RESPONSIBLE

ENCOUNTER God's Word in a Youth Bible study group

Teaching-learning approaches for helping youth:
• Get started into the session

• Get into the Truth

• Get the Truth into us

CONTINUE teaching-learning in daily living and family relationships

---

PRAYER CONCERNS

PREPARE the ministry environment for spiritual transformation

(10 min.) **FOCUS** on the Mission

(25 min.) **FOCUS** on Relationships

(25 min.) **FOCUS** on Bible Study
As a youth leader, how does this Bible study address my life as I:
• Acknowledge Authority—*What authority guides my life for this issue?*

• Search the Truth—*What did God say in the Bible?*

• Discover the Truth—*What abiding truth is the Holy Spirit teaching me?*

• Personalize the Truth—*What is the Holy Spirit teaching me about thinking, feeling, and living today?*

• Struggle with the Truth—*What conflict is in my heart?*

• Believe the Truth—*What do I need to change: mind, values, the way I live?*

• Obey the Truth—*How much will I obey the Holy Spirit?*

APPROACHES TO LEARNING & TEACHING FOR YOUTH*

RELATIONAL — Barnabas	MUSICAL — David	LOGICAL — Paul	NATURAL — David	PHYSICAL — Ezekiel	REFLECTIVE — Mary	VISUAL — John	VERBAL — Solomon
Learners Clarify— Leaders can ask youth, "What does this mean to you?"	**Learners Listen—** Leaders can play a contemporary Christian song and ask youth to listen to what the song says.	**Learners Organize—** Leaders can ask youth, "How can we address this problem? What can we do, who can do it, and when?"	**Learners Dig/Touch—** Leaders can introduce youth to the role of the sacrificial lamb by letting them observe a live lamb.	**Learners Touch—** Leaders can ask youth to join hands to form a circle to symbolize unity.	**Learners Meditate—** Leaders can encourage youth to think about things for which they are thankful.	**Learners Create a Montage—** Leaders can ask youth to create a montage from magazine photographs of people with great needs.	**Learners Listen—** Leaders can tell youth the story of Mary and Martha.
Learners Affirm— Leaders can encourage a youth to write a note to an adult who has been a help and support to them.	**Learners Record—** Leaders can provide a cassette recorder for youth to record songs, choral readings, and so forth.	**Learners Compare/Contrast—** Leaders can guide youth to contrast the fruit of the Spirit with the acts of the sinful nature.	**Learners Sort/Classify—** Leaders can ask youth to separate items into what God made and what people have made.	**Learners Recreate—** Leaders can guide youth to build a rock altar (like Jacob did) to mark a commitment they made to follow God.	**Learners Evaluate Themselves—** Leaders can ask youth to identify one weakness in their prayer lives.	**Learners Observe—** Leaders can direct youth to watch a videotaped case study, following this with a discussion or written response.	**Learners Paraphrase—** Leaders can ask youth to rewrite and tell the parable of the lost coins in a modern-day version.
Learners Empathize— Leaders can ask youth: "How do you think Jonathan felt knowing David would be king and not him?"	**Learners Sing—** Leaders can lead youth in singing "Awesome God" as a response to Psalm 8.	**Learners Reason—** Leaders can ask youth to respond to a series of if/then statements.	**Learners Observe—** Leaders can ask youth to observe a scientific demonstration and explain how it shows order in the universe.	**Learners Act/Dramatize—** Leaders can ask youth to act out a role play that demonstrates the principle of forgiveness.	**Learners Contemplate—** Leaders can ask youth to consider possible results of a particular mistake in their lives.	**Learners Diagram—** Leaders can ask youth to sketch what they think the temple might have looked like based on the Bible's descriptions of the temple.	**Learners List—** Leaders can ask youth to make a list of the Ten Commandments.
Learners Mediate— Leaders can ask youth to role play a conflict and discuss how to resolve the conflict.	**Learners Compose—** Leaders can ask youth to compose a song or rap that expresses the truth of the focal passage.	**Learners Analyze—** Leaders can ask youth, "Why do people act that way? What happens to a Christian who continues to act that way?"	**Learners Protect—** Leaders can guide youth to create and implement a project that reflects Christian stewardship of creation.	**Learners Move—** Leaders can ask youth to move to the appropriate agree/disagree poster, based on their opinions of certain statements.	**Learners Log—** Leaders can have youth track the amount of time they spend this week watching television and in prayer.	**Learners Draw/Illustrate—** Leaders can instruct youth to illustrate on a large sheet of paper areas where youth often feel tempted.	**Learners Write Ideas—** Leaders can ask youth to write a note to a senior adult member of the church.
Learners Question— Leaders can encourage youth to ask one another how they would respond to the case study.	**Learners Evaluate Music—** Leaders can ask youth to describe how the music made them feel.	**Learners Evaluate—** Leaders can show a video and ask youth to identify appropriate and inappropriate responses of characters to various situations.	**Learners Reflect—** Leaders can help youth identify principles of science that point to an orderly Creator.	**Learners Create—** Leaders can instruct youth to use chenille strips and create something that symbolizes something they can do for God.	**Learners Write in Journals—** Leaders can guide youth to keep a journal on ways they have experienced God's presence during the week.	**Learners Demonstrate—** Leaders can ask youth to show the results of their work during the class time.	**Learners Use Humor/Stories—** Leaders can ask youth to give humorous examples similar to Jesus' example of the plank and speck of dust.
Learners Respond— Leaders can instruct youth to list ways they could help a local ministry or mission project.	**Learners Respond to Music—** Leaders can ask youth to decide how music influences them.	**Learners Rank—** Leaders can ask youth to compare items and list them in order of their importance.	**Learners Collect/Display—** Leaders can ask youth to bring examples of environmental pollution.	**Learners Manipulate—** Leaders can instruct youth to rearrange the letters each of them is holding to create the Key Verse.	**Learners Study—** Leaders can ask youth to read the Focal Passage and answer questions about it.	**Learners Propose—** Leaders can ask youth to describe what they think Jesus might have seen when He looked out over the crowds while He hung on the cross.	**Learners Report—** Leaders can instruct youth to research the meaning of key words used in a passage and report findings to the class.
Learners Discuss— Leaders can guide youth to discuss possible consequences of disobeying those in authority.	**Learners Play Instruments—** Leaders can encourage youth to play instruments and lead the group in singing choruses.	**Learners Classify—** Leaders can display pictures of youth in different situations and direct youth to tell which pictures show ministry in action.	**Learners Identify—** Leaders can ask youth to clip photos or illustrations of items discovered in Holy Land excavations.	**Learners Play in Sports—** Leaders can encourage youth to use a basketball game to exhibit Christlikeness and open the door to witnessing.	**Learners Personalize—** Leaders can ask youth to assume the role of a biblical character in a given situation and identify how the person might have responded.	**Learners Paint—** Leaders can guide youth to design and paint a "billboard" that presents the gospel.	**Learners Label—** Leaders can call out various things and direct youth to say if they are wants or needs.
Learners Dialogue— Leaders can ask youth open-ended questions like, "How would you complete this sentence?"	**Learners Adapt/Create—** Leaders can direct youth to create new verses to a chorus that expresses things for which they are thankful.	**Learners Graph—** Leaders can guide youth to make a graph of their lives, showing high and low points in their walk with Christ.	**Learners Plant/Cultivate—** Leaders can lead youth to discuss the nature of faith by planting seeds and watching their growth over the months.	**Learners Display—** Leaders can ask youth to bring seemingly unrelated items to assemble in class to show how parts become the whole.	**Learners Intuit—** Leaders can ask youth to consider what God is directing them to do as a result of this study.	**Learners Storyboard—** Leaders can guide youth to create a six-panel cartoon that gives the main action of the story.	**Learners Recite—** Leaders can assign a psalm for youth to use in developing a dramatic monologue or responsive reading.

YOUTH INFORMATION SHEET | GETTING TO KNOW ME

Name: _____

Address: _____

City: _____ State: _____ Zip: _____ Phone: _____

E-mail: _____ Birthday: _____ Grade: _____ School: _____

Parent's Names: _____

Brothers, Sisters, and Pets (names and ages): _____

_____

My interests (Music, sports, hobbies, drama, etc.): _____

_____

School activities you participate in: _____

_____

Favorite TV shows/movies/singers/groups, etc.: _____

Have you accepted Christ? Yes _____ No _____ Have you been baptized? Yes _____ No _____

Church member? _____ Where? _____

Just for fun:
Please rank the following reasons in order with 1 being the most important reason, 2 being the next most important, and so forth. Your top 3 is enough. I come to Sunday School because:
___ My parents make me.
___ To be with my friends at church or a friend invited me.
___ As a family, we always come, and being a part of my family is important to me.
___ I want to study and learn the Bible.
___ I sense that adult leaders care about me, or an adult invited me.
___ Other:

Check one or more ways you like to learn:
___ Work in groups or serve people (relational)   ___ Sing, play, or listen to music (musical)
___ Solve problems, question, or reason (logical)   ___ Be out-of-doors, observe creation (natural)
___ Do drama, sports, or dance (physical)   ___ Work alone or think deeply (reflective)
___ Draw or make designs (visual)   ___ Write, speak, or read (verbal)

One of my favorite places is _____.

I am proud of _____.

I wish I could _____.

My favorite snacks are _____.

My favorite way to spend a day is _____.

I can make Sunday School better by _____.

THREE ESSENTIAL BEST PRACTICES OF BIBLE TEACHING FOR SPIRITUAL TRANSFORMATION

PREPARE
the ministry environment

Sunday School Leadership Meeting
- Focus on the Mission
- Focus on Relationships
- Focus on Bible Study

Personal Bible Study

ENCOUNTER
God's Word in a Bible Study group

Acknowledge Authority
(control)

Search the Truth
(content)

Discover the Truth
(concept)

Personalize the Truth
(context)

Struggle with the Truth
(conflict)

Believe the Truth
(conviction)

Obey the Truth
(conduct)

CONTINUE
Teaching-learning
in daily living and family relationships

Spiritual transformation is God's work of changing a believer into the likeness of Jesus by creating a new identity in Christ and by empowering a lifelong relationship of love, trust, and obedience to glorify God.

TEACHING PLAN
FOR *TEACHING YOUTH: LEADERS, LESSONS, AND LIFESTYLES*

By Bill Craig

Use this teaching plan as a starting point for planning learning experiences for leaders in Youth Sunday School. Determine the best schedule for training. Each of the ten suggestions in this plan is designed to be 15 minutes long. Use one step per week for ten weeks during your Sunday School Leadership meeting, or plan a two and one-half-hour training event to cover the entire plan at once. Be a model teacher for the leaders you are training by applying the principles from this book as you teach.

PREPARATION

For step 1: Provide a spiral notepad (journal) for each leader and copies of *Teaching Youth: Leaders, Lessons and Lifestyles.*

For step 2: Provide some teen clothing, a music CD, a telephone, and a school textbook. Have on hand large sheets of paper, felt-tip markers, copies of class rolls; duplicate copies of the list of assets found on pages 94-95 of *Teaching Youth.*

For step 3: Prepare a poster with guidelines for teaching for spiritual transformation from page 28 of *Teaching Youth.*

For step 4: Provide copies of each class roll; copies of curriculum materials; prepare three sentence strips that read: *Prepare the ministry environment, Encounter God's Word,* and *Continue in daily living and family responsibilities* and post them on a focal wall in random order.

For step 5: Provide copies of curriculum materials and art supplies.

For step 6: Provide copies of curriculum materials; prepare matching cards of the Seven Bible Teaching Elements by writing the seven C words on one set of cards (*control, content, concept,* etc.) and the definitions that match those words on another set of cards. (See pages 37-39.)

For step 7: Using posterboard or heavy paper, make eight placards—on each, write one of the eight learning style approaches (*relational, musical, logical, etc.*) from chapter 6.

For step 8: Duplicate copies of the Youth Sunday School Plan Sheet from the appendix of *Teaching Youth* and provide copies of curriculum.

For step 9: Provide a large sheet of paper

For step 10: Make a set of five jot sheets. On each one, write the first letter or word of one of the five *continue* strategies found in chapter 12 of *Teaching Youth.*

PROCEDURE

Step 1.—Why do you teach Youth Sunday School?
Distribute notepads, or some other type of journal, and explain that during the next few weeks (or throughout this conference) leaders are to become

investigative reporters seeking to uncover the truth about teaching youth in Sunday School. Direct leaders to work together in pairs to interview each other by asking the question: *Why do you teach Youth Sunday School?* Ask leaders to record their interviews in their notebooks. Call for reports. Ask a previously enlisted worker to share a testimony about why he or she teaches Youth Sunday School.

Distribute copies of *Teaching Youth: Leaders, Lessons, and Lifestyles*. Say: There are many reasons people give for teaching youth. One significant reason is to help youth experience spiritual transformation—to help youth have an encounter with God through Bible study during which they may be transformed into the likeness of Jesus.

Ask pairs of leaders to work together again to scan chapter 1 to discover Scripture passages that identify reasons we teach youth. Ask them to consider whether the Scripture they find speaks more to *preparing* to teach, the Bible study *encounter*, or the *continuing* effect of the Bible study lesson. Call for reports.

Video Option: Show first segment of the video where Alis and Ben are discussing the meaning of *transformation*.

Step 2.—Who do you teach in Youth Sunday School?
Divide leaders into four teams and give each team a large sheet of paper and a marker. Say: We're going to research chapter 2 to discover more about the *who?* of Youth Sunday School. Give team 1 an article of teen clothing and ask them to prepare a brief summary of the physical characteristics of teens (younger and older). Give team 2 a music CD and ask them to prepare a summary of the emotional development of teens. Give team 3 the telephone and ask them to prepare a brief summary of the social development of teens. Give team 4 the textbook and ask them to prepare a brief summary of the mental development of teens. Call for reports, and conclude by sharing insights into the spiritual development of teens. Remind leaders to take notes on their investigators' notepads. Ask: How do these descriptions "fit" the teens in your class?

Say: Researchers have discovered that when certain assets are a part of teens' lives they are more likely to succeed in life. Distribute copies of the assets listed in chapter 10 or display them on a large sheet of paper. Also distribute class rolls to each leader. Guide leaders to consider the lists of assets and the teens in their classes. Ask: What one or two assets could you focus on adding to the teens in your class? How will adding each asset foster an environment for spiritual growth in those teenagers?

Step 3.—What are we doing in Youth Sunday School?
Divide leaders into two teams for a debate. Direct team 1 to develop arguments to support the statement: *I teach the Bible.* Direct team 2 to develop arguments to support the statement: *I teach youth.* Allow teams to present arguments in support of their statements. Following the debate, ask: Is there a better statement of what we do in Sunday School? If no one suggests it, point out that what we are doing in Sunday School is actually teaching youth the Bible. Share, from chapter 3, the definition of Great Commission teaching: Christ as the authority; people as the focus; obedience as the goal; God's Word as the content; and Christ's presence as the power (p. 28, *Teaching Youth*).

Ask leaders to listen for the key elements in 2 Timothy 2:15 as you read

aloud that verse. Call for leaders to share the key elements they heard and supplement their responses with information from pages 29-30 of the book.

Display the poster on which you have written the guidelines for teaching for spiritual transformation. Ask each leader to select one of the guidelines and share how he or she believes it contributes to teaching for spiritual transformation.

Step 4.—How do we prepare for Youth Sunday School? (Part 1)

Call for a volunteer to place in order the three sentence strips on the focal wall. Point out that these are the three essentials necessary for Bible teaching that leads to spiritual transformation.

Explain that you are going to focus on one aspect of preparing the ministry environment by conducting a portion of a leadership team meeting. Direct leaders to find the leadership meeting suggestions on the first page of a Bible study session in their leader guides (or use a copy of a sample lesson if leader guides are not available). Ask: What are the three items we focus on in a leadership meeting? Use the suggestions provided in the lesson to conduct a portion of a leadership meeting—at least the sections called "Focusing on the Mission" and "Focusing on Relationships."

Video Option: Show the Sunday School Leadership Meeting from segment 2 of the video.

Step 5.—How do we prepare for Youth Sunday School? (Part 2)

Divide leaders into two or three teams as you lead them to examine another aspect of *preparing*. Direct team 1 to review the "Personal Bible Study" section of their leader guides and to be prepared to explain the features of the section to the other team. Ask team 1 to prepare an artistic display that represents their favorite feature of the "Personal Bible Study." Direct team 2 to overview the "encounter" and "options" pages of the lesson and to be prepared to overview the features of those sections. Ask team 2 (or team 3, if you have one) to prepare to lead one short teaching activity suggested in the "encounter" pages. Complete this activity by reviewing how these sections are a vital part of a leader's *preparation* for a good Bible study.

Video option: Show the video segment where Lynn (the teacher) explains that being a Sunday School teacher means he or she must experience spiritual transformation in their own life.

Step 6.—How do we encounter God's Word in Youth Sunday School? (Part 1)

Point out the *encounter* sentence strip from step 4 as you guide leaders to consider one aspect of *encountering* God's Word in Bible study. Distribute the matching cards by giving the C words to half the group and giving the definitions to the other half. Ask leaders to match the C words with the correct definitions. As they match the cards, briefly discuss the biblical process of instruction as presented in chapter 4 of *Teaching Youth*.

Step 7.—How do we encounter God's Word in Youth Sunday School? (Part 2)

Distribute placards identifying the eight learning style approaches and mention that you are examining another aspect of *encountering* God's Word in Bible study. Direct leaders to work in pairs (or alone) to use the book to review the definition of their assigned learning style approach. Guide leaders to present their assigned definition to the group, and to demonstrate that approach if time permits. Ask leaders to identify which approaches they prefer for themselves. Finally, ask the leaders to select one learning approach they are most uncomfortable using and describe why it is an effective approach with some teens. Refer leaders to chapter 6 as they complete the assignment.

Video option: Show the segment that was filmed during an actual Sunday School Bible study session. Ask conferees if they can identify some learning approaches that were used or suggest places where others might have been used in the teaching situation.

Step 8.—How do we encounter God's Word in Youth Sunday School? (Part 3)

Explain that you are discovering another aspect of encountering God's Word in this activity—developing a plan for a Bible study encounter. Distribute copies of the plan sheet. Point out that the Youth Sunday School Plan Sheet has the seven elements listed under the *prepare* section. Ask: Why? (*to help leaders experience spiritual transformation before they teach youth*) Guide workers to complete the plan sheet for an upcoming Bible study session. Draw on information from chapters 7 and 8 as you lead this step.

Step 9.—How do we continue Youth Sunday School? (Part 1)

Display the *continue* sentence strip from step 4 and the 7 Bible teaching element matching cards from step 6. Ask: Which of the 7 Bible teaching elements are you likely to accomplish during an hour of Bible study? Which ones likely cannot be accomplished in the classroom? Explain that the process of struggling with the truth, and believing and obeying the truth often are accomplished only in the context of a Christian's daily walk. Guide leaders to brainstorm ways they can continue teaching lessons beyond the Bible study encounter. Record their responses on paper. Ask: What can we do to encourage accountability? How can we continue lessons in the families of the youth we teach? Refer to chapters 9 and 11 as you discuss continuing the lesson.

Video option: Show the parts of segment 2 that picture Lynn studying and praying, worshiping with youth, participating in visitation, and at a fellowship.

Step 10.—How do we continue Youth Sunday School? (Part 2)

Divide conferees into five teams and assign each team one of the *continue* strategies found in chapter 12 of *Teaching Youth*. Give each team a jot sheet and direct teams to prepare to explain to the rest of the group how to implement their assigned principle. After all have shared, guide leaders to make a commitment by completing the following sentence and writing it on their jot sheet: I will continue next week's Bible study by . . . .

Video option: Show the closing segment with Ben and Alis where Alis has expressed interest in becoming a Christian.

Close in prayer that this conference will lead to many teenagers experiencing spiritual transformation.

TEACHING PLAN

CHRISTIAN GROWTH STUDY PLAN

Preparing Christians to Serve

In the Christian Growth Study Plan (formerly Church Study Course), this book *Teaching Youth: Leaders, Lessons, and Lifestyles* is a resource for course credit in seven Leadership and Skill Development diploma plans. To receive credit, read the book, complete the learning activities, show your work to your pastor, a staff member or church leader, then complete the following information. This page may be duplicated. Send the completed page to:

Christian Growth Study Plan

127 Ninth Avenue, North

Nashville, TN 37234-0117

Fax: (615) 251-5067

For more information, refer to the current Christian Growth Study Plan Catalog. Your church office may have a copy. If not, request a free copy from the Christian Growth Study Plan office (615/251-2525).

COURSE CREDIT INFORMATION

Please check the appropriate box indicating the course(s) you want to apply this credit. You may check more than one box.

❑ Teaching Youth (LS-0027, Youth Ministers, Sunday School, Discipleship Training, Acteens, Youth on Mission)

❑ Guiding an Age Group in Vacation Bible School (LS-0056, Sunday School)

❑ Teaching Persons with Special Needs (LS-0106, Sunday School)

PARTICIPANT INFORMATION

Social Security Number (USA Only)	Personal CGSP Number	Date of Birth (Mo., Day, Yr.)
| | | – | | | – | | | |	| | | | – | | | – | | |	| | – | | – | |

Name (First, MI, Last) ❑Mr. ❑Miss ❑Mrs. ❑		Home Phone
		| | | – | | | – | | |

Address (Street, Route, or P.O. Box)	City, State, or Province	Zip/Postal Code
		| | | | |

CHURCH INFORMATION

Church Name

Address (Street, Route, or P.O. Box)	City, State, or Province	Zip/Postal Code
		| | | | |

CHANGE REQUEST ONLY

❑Former Name

❑Former Address	City, State, or Province	Zip/Postal Code
		| | | | |

❑Former Church	City, State, or Province	Zip/Postal Code
		| | | | |

Signature of Pastor, Conference Leader, or Other Church Leader	Date

*New participants are requested but not required to give SS# and date of birth. Existing participants, please give CGSP# when using SS# for the first time. Thereafter, only one ID# is required. Mail To: Christian Growth Study Plan, 127 Ninth Ave., North, MSN 117, Nashville, TN 37234-0117. Fax: (615)251-5067